PVC+PIPE
ENGINEER

Brimming with creative inspiration, how-to projects, and useful information to enrich your everyday life, Quarto Knows is a favorite destination for those pursuing their interests and passions. Visit our site and dig deeper with our books into your area of interest: Quarto Creates, Quarto Cooks, Quarto Homes, Quarto Lives, Quarto Drives, Quarto Explores, Quarto Gifts, or Quarto Kids.

First Published in 2018
by Rockport Publishers, an imprint of
The Quarto Group,
100 Cummings Center, Suite 265-D
Beverly, MA 01915, USA.

T (978) 282-9590 F (978) 283-2742
QuartoKnows.com

Rockport Publishers titles are also available at discount for retail, wholesale, promotional, and bulk purchase. For details, contact the Special Sales Manager by email at specialsales@quarto.com or by mail at The Quarto Group, Attn: Special Sales Manager, 401 Second Avenue North, Suite 310, Minneapolis, MN 55401, USA.

10 9 8 7 6 5 4 3 2 1

ISBN: 978-1-63159-334-5

Library of Congress Cataloging-in-Publication Data is available

Design: Timothy Samara
Photography: Jordan Bunker

Printed in China

PVC+PIPE
ENGINEER

PUT TOGETHER COOL, EASY, MAKER-FRIENDLY STUFF

JORDAN BUNKER

ROCKPORT

CONTENTS

There was a time when PVC and iron pipe were hidden deep inside the crawlspaces in your house, carrying liquids and gases to and from sinks and appliances. But not any more! The straightforward, no nonsense look of PVC and iron pipe has caught on with homeowners and earned a place in every room of the house (and the backyard, too).

—

The 17 projects in this book, ranging from wine racks to bed frames, and from showerheads to bike trailers, can all be made with parts you'll find at your local hardware store.

INTRODUCTION

**Ready? Clear some space,
get out your tools, and let's get to it!**

There are projects here for all skill levels.
Once you learn the basics of cutting and joining
iron pipe and PVC, you'll be surprised at how
easily even the big projects go together. Whether
you're building a superpowered water blaster,
a minimalist modern ceiling lamp, or even just a
simple candle holder, the illustrated how-to steps
in this book will show even first-time DIYers
how to build projects they're proud of.

I know, I know, you're eager to get started, but it's important to learn a bit about the materials you'll be working with first. Here, we'll cover the basic terminology, tools, and techniques that will prepare you for the projects to come. After reading this section, you'll have all of the information you need to avoid confusion, acquire the right tools, and build with confidence.

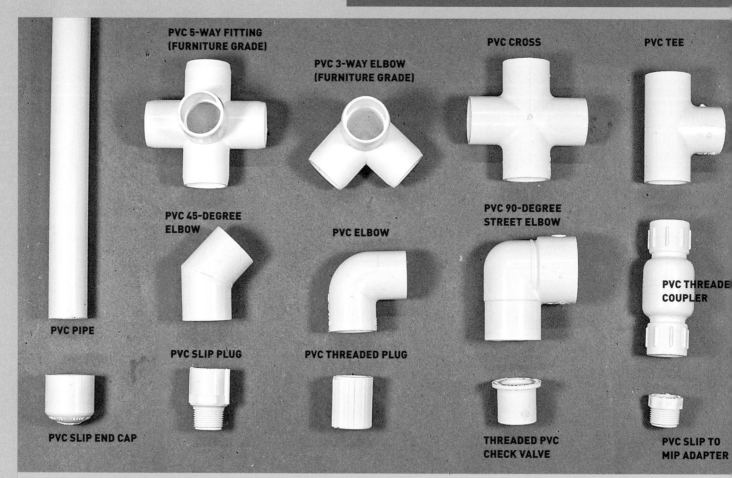

PVC 5-WAY FITTING (FURNITURE GRADE)

PVC 3-WAY ELBOW (FURNITURE GRADE)

PVC CROSS

PVC TEE

PVC 45-DEGREE ELBOW

PVC ELBOW

PVC 90-DEGREE STREET ELBOW

PVC THREADED COUPLER

PVC PIPE

PVC SLIP PLUG

PVC THREADED PLUG

PVC SLIP END CAP

THREADED PVC CHECK VALVE

PVC SLIP TO MIP ADAPTER

PVC PIPE

Nothing can make you lose enthusiasm for a project faster than getting home from the hardware store and realizing that the things you bought aren't quite right for the project at hand. If you've never worked with PVC (polyvinyl chloride) pipe before, you'll do yourself a favor to learn a little bit about it before you shell out your hard-earned dollars for supplies. Here are a few PVC pipe facts and pointers to help you get started.

In its humble history, PVC pipe was designed for use in plumbing for passing wastewater along to the sewer. That's what it's designed to do, but it can also be used as a light-duty structural component and for (somewhat) high-pressure applications, too.

PVC comes in different sizes. The listed diameter of PVC pipe corresponds to its internal diameter (ID). This is a nominal measurement, that is, "in name only," not an actual measurement. Be sure to note what diameter PVC pipe is called for in a project, and make sure the diameter of the pipe matches the diameter of the fitting you purchase. It's a good idea to test your fittings on your pipe while you're at the store, just to be sure.

You may have heard of pipes having a "schedule," as in schedule 40 or schedule 80. A PVC pipe's schedule is related to the thickness of the pipe's walls. The higher the schedule number, the thicker the pipe walls. In this book, we'll deal exclusively with schedule 40 PVC pipe.

FITTINGS

PVC fittings are designed to fit over the ends of pipe, allowing two or more pieces to join in different directions or to cap off the ends. Thanks to the complexity of modern plumbing systems, PVC fittings come in hundreds of shapes and sizes, designed for all diameter of pipe. There are even companies that make nonplumbing PVC fittings specifically for making furniture. Not surprisingly, these are known as "furniture-grade" fittings. Whenever possible in this book, I'll stick to the more common plumbing fittings, as they're more likely to be found in your local hardware store. On those rare occasions when only a specialized fitting will do, I'll provide as much information as possible about it and where you can get it.

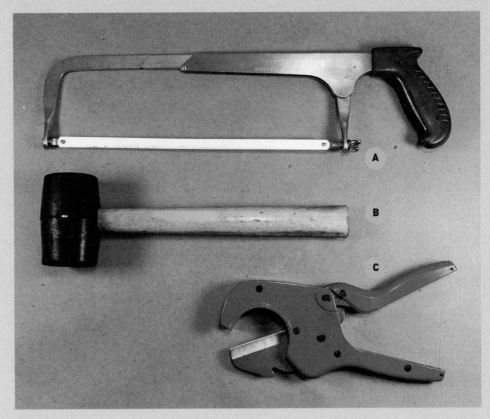

CUTTING

When it comes to cutting PVC pipe, there are a couple of options: a hacksaw or a tubing cutter.

Hacksaw. I like this option because most everyone with a workbench and toolbox already has a hacksaw **[A]**. While it may not leave the cleanest edge, any burrs and marks that a hacksaw leaves behind can be smoothed with a file and sandpaper. A hacksaw also offers great versatility, allowing you to cut plastic pipe of any diameter at any angle, or in any required shape.
—
Tubing cutter. This tool is designed specifically for cutting plastic tubing. It's quick, efficient, leaves a very clean edge, and it doesn't leave any PVC dust behind. However, most tubing cutters will cut only relatively narrow

diameter pipe: up to 1½" or 2" (40 or 50 mm). Beyond that, you'll need a saw. Additionally, a tubing cutter **[C]** is typically used to cut pipe perpendicular to its length, so fancy angled cuts are, again, best left to the hacksaw.

ASSEMBLING

When test-fitting pipe into PVC fittings, you'll discover it sometimes helps to give things a little friendly percussive force. For this, I recommend a rubber mallet **[B]**. Its soft rubber end has enough give to prevent damage to the PVC, and it will help seat the pieces firmly. This is especially useful on large projects.

GLUING

The process of gluing pieces of PVC pipe into fittings is solvent-based rather than adhesive. First, to prepare the plastic for bonding, you'll apply a primer to the outside end of the pipe and to the interior of the fitting. Then you apply cement over the primer and assemble the pieces. The cement melts the plastic slightly so that, when it sets up, the pipe and fitting become a single piece of PVC—a very strong bond. The primer and cement are frequently sold together in packs. Each chemical has its own dauber attached to the lid.

Many of the PVC primers and cements that you'll find at the hardware store have brightly colored dyes added to them, which makes it easier to verify that joints have been glued. If you're worried about the appearance of the project, and you don't plan on painting it, I recommend finding transparent primer and cement to keep your project looking clean.

DRILLING

PVC is a soft plastic, and drilling it is fairly straightforward. Most drill bits made for metal or wood can be used on PVC without any issue. However, there is one trick. Since pipe is round, it can be difficult to get a hole started. Before starting a hole, it's a good idea to make a small divot with a nail or prick-punch, so that the drill bit has a starting point and won't slide. I also recommend clamping the pipe in a vice, or at the very least, attaching a long clamp and holding it with your nondrill hand to keep the pipe from rolling.

CLEANING

PVC is typically white, which means that dirt and all manner of scuff marks show up easily. Additionally, the PVC you buy at the hardware store is often printed with text that identifies its properties. There are two good ways to remove the unsightly text and marks: acetone or sanding.

—

Acetone. Use an acetone-dampened rag to wipe away the text. The acetone will also remove a small amount of the surface of the pipe, but not enough to be noticeable.

—

Sanding. Sanding is a great way to remove dirt, text, and anything else that you don't want showing up on your pipe. I recommend a 120 to 220 grit sandpaper to remove most offending marks, and then finishing with 320 grit to smooth the surface.

PAINTING

If you're planning on building a number of the PVC-pipe projects in this book (and I hope you are), you'll probably want to add a bit of color to at least some of them. That's easy to do using spray paints that are specially formulated for use on plastic. Clean and sand the pipe and fittings as mentioned previously, but stop after the 220 grit sanding: the rough surface will help the paint stick a bit better. Spray a light coat of paint over your project, wait 10 to 15 minutes for the coat to dry, and repeat until you have the look you desire.

SAFETY FIRST

As with any chemical, care should be taken when using chemicals such as acetone and PVC glue, so wear safety glasses and latex gloves. Also make sure that you are in a well-ventilated area (preferably outdoors) when using the glue, as the fumes can be quite strong.

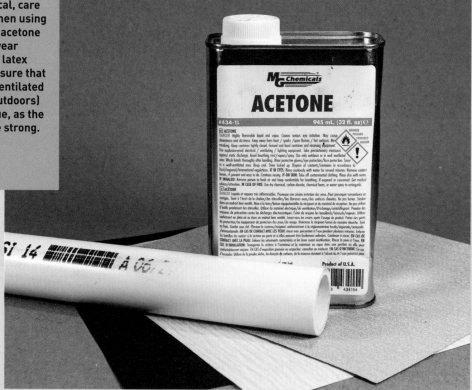

TEE

90-DEGREE ELBOW

FLOOR FLANGE

REDUCING COUPLER

90-DEGREE ELBOW WITH SIDE OUTLET

UNION

END CAP

CLOSE NIPPLE

COUPLER

PIPE NIPPLE

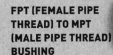

FPT (FEMALE PIPE THREAD) TO MPT (MALE PIPE THREAD) BUSHING

MALLEABLE IRON PIPE

Iron pipe is a wonderfully versatile material. It's inexpensive and sturdy, withstands high heat and pressure, and when liberated from its original purpose in plumbing, it can be used in all kinds of structural applications. As handy as it is, if you're working with iron pipe for the first time, there are a few things you should know:

The two types of iron pipe you'll see at a hardware store are black iron pipe, which is a matte black color, and galvanized pipe, which is a shiny gray metallic color. In this book, I use mostly black iron pipe, but that's primarily an aesthetic choice. Feel free to substitute other pipe types if you want. Iron pipe is commonly available in the plumbing section of a hardware store, and is typically found in ½", ¾", and 1" (15, 20, and 25 mm) sizes. Projects in this book will focus mainly on those sizes. Note that these sizes are nominal, that is "in name only." They are not actual inside or outside diameters.

FITTINGS

To join one piece of pipe to another, you'll need a fitting on the end. As with PVC, there are dozens of fitting types to choose from, but the most important factor is to make sure that the diameter and thread of the pipe matches the diameter and thread of the fitting—this allows the fitting to screw onto the end of the pipe securely and easily. Fittings are prethreaded when you buy them.

Standard lengths of iron pipe are often available prethreaded too, but a piece of pipe cut to a custom length will need to have the threading cut into it. Information about that appears below. Most fittings you'll find at the hardware store are designed for plumbing and gas purposes, but there are specialized furniture fittings available, too. When a project in this book requires one of these, it will be noted as such in the materials list.

CUTTING

As you might suspect, iron pipe is a bit more difficult to cut than PVC. Thankfully, there are a number of cutting options to choose from.
—
Hardware Store. Most places that sell iron pipe have the capability to cut it for you. This is the option I recommend: It saves time and effort. Be sure to have the exact lengths and diameters of each piece of pipe you need written down.

Hacksaw [A]. This is the most versatile option: You can cut pipe at any angle you please. It is also the most labor intensive (been to the gym lately?), and requires the use of a vise to clamp the pipe in place while cutting.
—
Pipe Cutter [B]. This tool uses a cutting wheel that clamps around the pipe and is rotated around it, tightening with each revolution. The cutting wheel cuts into the pipe, eventually slicing through to the inside. This is a very precise way to get straight and even cuts.

THREADING

Freshly cut pipe isn't very useful until you add threads—cut grooves, as on a screw top—to the end of it. Most pipe and fittings that you'll find at the hardware store have the standard thread profile of the National Pipe Thread taper (NPT).
—
NPT threads come in MPT (Male Pipe Taper) and FPT (Female Pipe Taper). Male threads are on the outside of the fitting or pipe; female threads are on the inside of the fitting or pipe. Adding threads to a pipe is done using a tool called a die, which cuts into the metal as you spin it. Most large hardware stores have threading machines: If you are purchasing your pipe and having it cut to length there, ask them to put threads on it, too. You can also buy a die set and do the threading yourself. This is only worthwhile if you are doing a lot of work with metal pipe: Die sets can be pricey.

ASSEMBLING

If you can turn a doorknob, you can assemble pipe fittings. Getting a pipe to thread into a fitting is usually pretty easy. But if you want a fitting joint to be especially tight, you'll want to use a pipe wrench [C] and/or a set of groove-joint pliers [D] to really cinch it. Most projects also require that fittings be tightened to a specific angle, which can be difficult to do without a tool to grab parts securely. If you're worried about marring the surface of the metal, simply wrap duct tape around the teeth of your pliers or wrench. It's not a pretty solution, but it is an effective one.

CLEANING AND CARE

Working with iron pipe is messy business. When you purchase most black pipe and fittings, they're covered with a thin coating of grease that keeps the metal from rusting. I recommend removing that coating before you start building. Wipe down the pipe with a rag [E] and some mineral spirits [F]. After cleaning the metal, use another rag to rub paste wax [G] over the surface of the pipe, which will protect the metal from rust, but won't leave a greasy mess. Even after cleaning the metal, it's a good idea to wear gloves when assembling your projects, as the threads can be quite sharp.

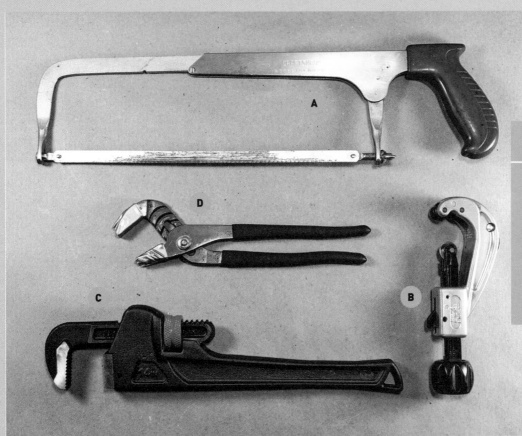

NOTE

Regardless of what method you choose, be sure always to deburr a freshly cut edge with a file or deburring tool before you thread it.

PIPE SIZES: STANDARD TO METRIC

PVC and malleable iron pipe have size names that only roughly correspond to an actual inside diameter. The metric name is therefore not a true conversion, but what is labeled as "diameter nominal" or DN.
—
Here are corresponding sizes for the materials used in this book:

Nominal Pipe Size	Diameter Nominal
⅛"	6 mm
¼"	8 mm
½"	15 mm
¾"	20 mm
1"	25 mm
1¼"	32 mm
1½"	40 mm
2"	50 mm
3"	80 mm
6"	150 mm

TERMS USED IN THIS BOOK

Here are some abbreviations and terms that are used throughout this book:

ID   Inside Diameter—an actual measurement of the inside of a tube

OD   Outside Diameter—actual measurement of the outside of a tube

NPT   National Pipe Taper—the standard for threads on malleable iron pipe, which have a slight taper

FPT   Female Pipe Taper—tapered threads on the interior of a fitting

MPT   Male Pipe Taper—tapered threads on the exterior of a pipe or fitting

Slip   A PVC fitting that has no threads

EMT   Electric Metallic Tube—the tubing that wiring is housed in. This book uses the mounting straps for EMT.

IP, IPS   Iron Pipe Straight—nontapered threads

MIP/FIP   Male Iron Pipe and Female Iron Pipe straight threaded fittings, typically found on brass or copper

RESOURCES

PVC AND IRON PIPE

Shop at your local hardware store. If you're buying in large quantities, you can also check plumbing and HVAC supply stores, which may offer more affordable prices.

FURNITURE-GRADE PVC FITTINGS

If you have a hard time finding furniture grade PVC fittings at local stores, it's fairly easy to find them for sale online.

LAMP PARTS

Many of the lamp parts used in this book can be found at your local hardware store. They will definitely be available at a lighting supply store.

YURT

As an alternative to taping the plastic into place, you can use special clips designed specifically for clipping plastic sheeting to PVC. You may be able to find them at a garden or greenhouse supply store. If not, the clips can be found online.

FOAM ROCKET LAUNCHER

The electronic irrigation valve and other electronic components can usually be found at a hardware store. If not, check out hobby shops or search online.

TOOLS

All of the tools used in this book can be found at hardware stores.

Who doesn't love a good gadget? With these three PVC projects, you can boost your phone's speakers, kick up the jams at your desk, and take a nice relaxing shower under a warm gentle rain. These projects are some of the simplest in the book, so they're a great place to start for quick and easy weekend fun!

GADGETS

PHONE AMPLIFIER

Is your phone's speaker a little lacking? Do you want to blast music, but don't want to spring for a powered amplifier? This quick project is all about making a passive amplifier for boosting the volume from phones with bottom-mounted speakers. The easy three-piece design accommodates a USB charging cable as well, so charging while listening is no problem.

TOOLS

MASKING TAPE

SMALL SHEET OF GLASS OR PLASTIC

MARKER

ROTARY TOOL WITH PLASTIC CUTTING DISC OR A DRILL WITH ⅛" (3 MM) DRILL BIT

ASSORTED METAL FILES

PVC PRIMER AND GLUE (OPTIONAL)

SANDPAPER (OPTIONAL)

SPRAY PAINT (OPTIONAL)

HOT GLUE GUN (OPTIONAL)

MATERIALS

ONE 1½" × 1½" × ½" (40 × 40 × 15 MM) PVC REDUCING TEE

TWO 1½" (40 MM) PVC 90-DEGREE STREET ELBOWS

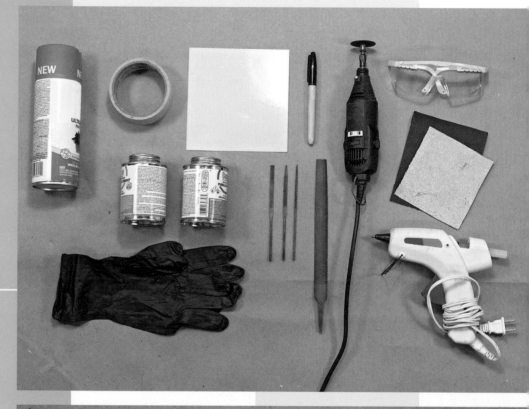

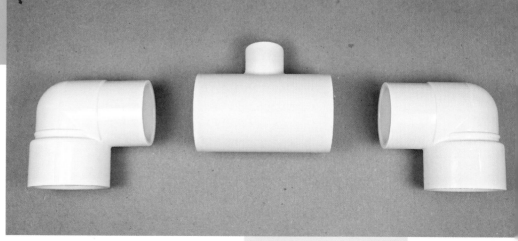

INSTRUCTIONS

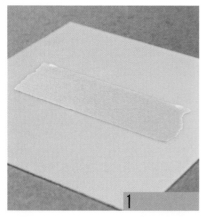

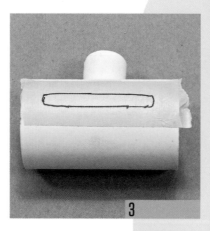

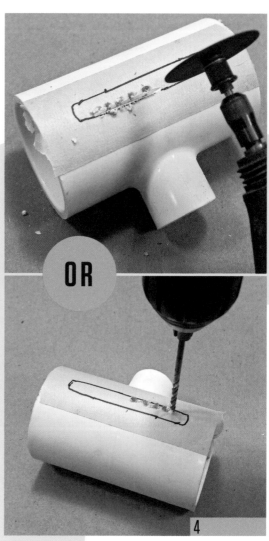

OR

1_Tear off a piece of masking tape a bit wider than your phone. Place it on a flat piece of plastic or glass. A windowpane will work just fine.

2_Hold the bottom of your phone to the piece of tape. Trace around it with a marker.

3_Place the PVC reducing tee on a flat surface with the smaller middle segment facing away from you. Peel the piece of tape from the glass and place it on top of the tee. Be sure to center the outline you drew as close to the middle as possible.

4_Using a rotary tool with a plastic-cutting disc, remove most of the material inside the outline. If you don't have a rotary tool, use a drill. Drill a series of holes, just inside the outline, all the way around to cut out the middle.

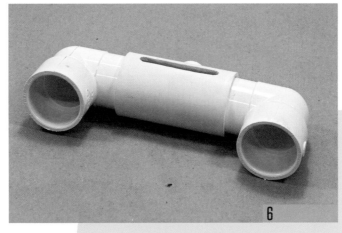

6

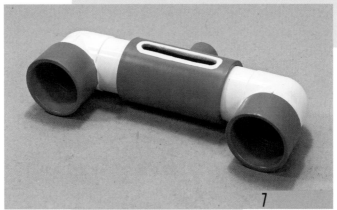

7

5

5 _ Remove the tape. Use files to smooth the inside edges of the phone-shaped hole. Make sure your phone fits (loosely). Keep filing as necessary.

6 _ Insert a 90-degree elbow on either side of the tee. If the elbows won't fit because your phone is in the way, remove the phone, reinsert the elbows. Mark, cut, and file the elbows as needed.

7 _ Glue the elbows into place if you like. Since the pieces don't really need to hold any weight, you can just leave them to friction fit if you prefer. You can also sand and paint the pieces if you have a color other than white in mind!

8

8 _ Finally, insert your phone and test it. If all is well, insert the charging cord through the middle segment of the tee in the back, pull the cord through to the desired length, then squirt some hot glue into the opening to keep it from pulling out.

SPEAKERS

There's nothing worse than a party without music, so crank up the volume with these awesome PVC speakers. The instructions and materials here are for building one speaker, but the pair is identical, so double the materials and follow the instructions again to make another when you're done with the first.

TOOLS

MARKER

HACKSAW

DRILL

$\frac{1}{16}$" (1.6 MM) DRILL BIT

$\frac{5}{32}$" (3.9 MM) DRILL BIT

MASKING TAPE

PHILLIPS SCREWDRIVER

WIRE STRIPPER

ELECTRICAL TAPE

TAPE MEASURE

SOLDERING IRON AND SOLDER
(OPTIONAL)

SANDPAPER AND SPRAY PAINT
(OPTIONAL)

PLIERS (OPTIONAL)

MATERIALS [FOR ONE SPEAKER]

1' TO 2' (30.5 TO 61 CM) OF
3" (80 MM) PVC PIPE

ONE 3" (7.5 CM) PVC 90-DEGREE ELBOW

ONE 3" (80 MM) ROUND FRAME
SPEAKER (I RECOMMEND MODEL
HIVI B3N)

FOUR #6 × $\frac{3}{4}$" (3 × 20 MM)
PHILLIPS SCREWS

SPEAKER WIRE, APPROXIMATELY
2' (61 CM)

ONE 3" (7.5 CM) ABS CLOSET FLANGE

TWO SPEAKER BINDING POSTS
(ONE RED, ONE BLACK)

ONE HANDFUL OF FIBER FILL

FOUR RUBBER FEET WITH NUTS
AND BOLTS (OPTIONAL)

INSTRUCTIONS

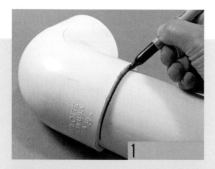

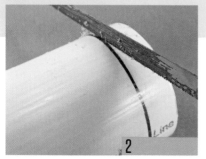

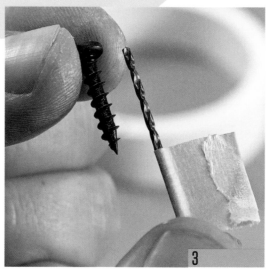

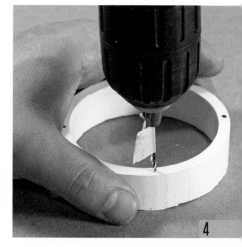

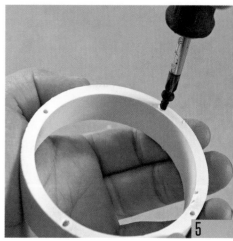

1_Insert one end of the pipe into the 90-degree elbow. With a marker, trace around the pipe along the edge of the elbow. Remove the pipe.

2_Cut the pipe along the tracing line. Place one of your speakers inside the ring. Center the speaker in the ring. Use the marker to mark the position of the four mounting holes in the speaker rim.

3_Hold one of the speaker mounting screws next to the $1/16$" (1.6 mm) drill bit to measure the depth for the holes. Wrap a piece of masking tape around the drill bit so you know when to stop drilling.

4_Carefully drill through the four marks in the rim. Drill the holes straight down to the depth of the tape. It's important that these holes are straight: An angled hole will cause the screw to poke out of the side of the ring. If you make a mistake, rotate the ring and repeat steps 3 and 4 and try again.

5_Insert a screw into each hole and run it all the way in to create threads inside the holes, then remove the screws.

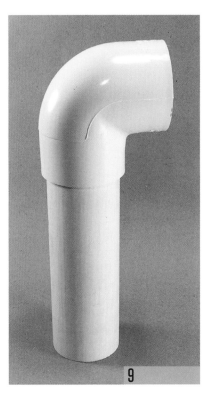

9 _ Decide how long you want the vertical section of the speaker to be. Cut a length of pipe to that measurement. Insert it into the elbow. (I cut mine to 10" [25.5 cm].)

6 _ Cut about 2" (61 cm) of speaker wire and strip about ½" (13 mm) off the end of each wire.

7 _ Wrap one wire around the positive (red) tab on the speaker and the other around the negative (black) tab. If you have a soldering iron, solder the wires into place. If you don't, do your best to twist the wires around the tabs so they won't come loose. When the wires are secured, wrap each connection with electrical tape to protect them. The speaker wire should have

one side that is marked with a line to differentiate it from the other. Make a note which tab it went to.

8 _ Run the speaker wires through the speaker ring. Line up the speaker with the holes you made earlier. If your speaker came with a foam sealing ring, make sure that it is inserted between the ring and the speaker. Secure the speaker in place with the screws.

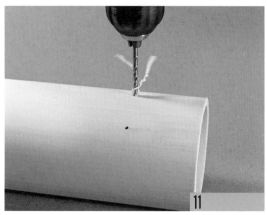

10 _ Insert the PVC pipe fully into the closet flange. Measure 1" (2.5 cm) from the edge of the flange and make two marks approximately 1½" (4 cm) away from each other. This will be where the binding posts will be inserted.

11 _ Remove the vertical pipe. Using the appropriately sized drill bit for your binding posts (I used ⁵/₃₂" [3.9 mm]), drill holes in the two marks you made in step 11. Test the binding posts in the holes to make sure they fit correctly.

12 _ If you want to paint your speakers, now is the time. Separate the elbow, vertical pipe, and flange. Sand them and spray paint them according to the directions on page 10. You might want to cover the sections of the vertical pipe that will be inside the flange and elbow with masking tape prior to painting, just to make sure there aren't any issues with inserting them later. Let the paint dry thoroughly, then reassemble the pieces before following the next steps.

13 _ Run the wires of the wired speaker through the elbow. Insert the ring into the elbow fully.

14 _ Run the speaker wires through the vertical section of the pipe and let them hang through the bottom. Rotate the pipe so that the holes for the binding posts are on the rear (pointing away from the speaker). Insert the pipe into the elbow.

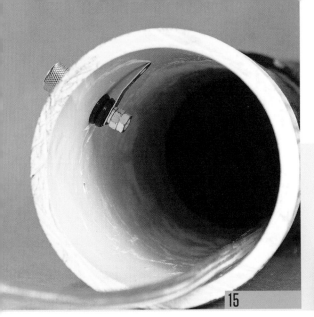

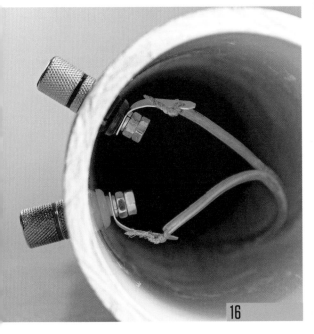

18 _ Finally, insert the vertical pipe into the flange, wire the speaker to your amplifier, and blast some music!

15 _ Remove the binding post nuts. Insert the binding posts into the holes in the pipe and secure them with the nuts. Use pliers to reach inside and tighten the nuts, if necessary.

16 _ Trim the speaker wire so it's just a bit longer than the pipe. Strip the ends. Wire the binding posts, taking note of which wire was which from step 7, and connecting black to black and red to red. Secure the wires with electrical tape.

17 _ Place a loose handful of the fiber fill inside the bottom of the pipe. This will help increase the apparent volume of the pipe, and can make the speaker sound better. If you like, attach four rubber feet to the bottom of the flange using adhesive tape or bolts and nuts through the flange holes.

RAINFALL SHOWER HEAD

Is your shower head a bit . . . lacking? If you've wanted to experience the glory of a full, warm rain in the comfort of your own shower, then this is the project for you. This quick build will help you design your own large luxury showerhead for the ultimate relaxing spray.

—

Some of the lengths of the materials necessary for this project depend on design decisions and ceiling heights, so it's a good idea to read through all the steps before determining how much of each material you need.

TOOLS

TAPE MEASURE

PERMANENT MARKER

PVC CUTTER OR HACKSAW

MASKING TAPE

DRILL

$\frac{1}{16}$" (1.6 MM) DRILL BIT

RUBBER MALLET

FLATHEAD SCREWDRIVER

PVC PRIMER AND GLUE
(and gloves for protection)

STUD FINDER

PENCIL

PLIERS

MATERIALS

10' (3 M) OF $\frac{1}{2}$" (15 MM) PVC PIPE

NINE $\frac{1}{2}$" (15 MM) PVC TEES

ONE $\frac{1}{2}$" (15 MM) PVC CROSS

FOUR $\frac{1}{2}$" (15 MM) PVC
90-DEGREE ELBOWS

ONE $\frac{1}{2}$" (15 MM) PVC SLIP
TO MIP ADAPTER

2' (61 CM) OF $\frac{5}{8}$" ID $\frac{7}{8}$" OD
(ID 16 MM OD 22 MM) VINYL TUBING

TWO STAINLESS STEEL PIPE
CLAMPS ($\frac{1}{2}$" TO 1$\frac{1}{4}$" [13 TO 31 MM])

FOUR EYE SCREWS WITH
$\frac{1}{2}$" (13 MM) THREAD

10' TO 12' (3 M TO 3.6 M) SINGLE JACK
CHAIN, GALVANIZED STEEL

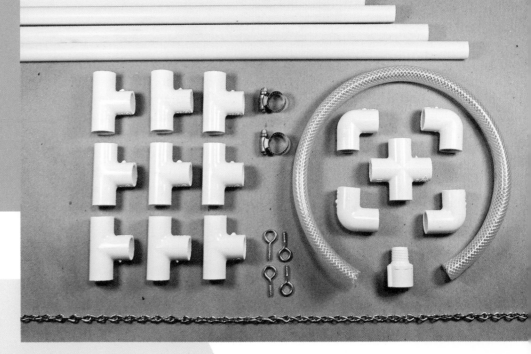

INSTRUCTIONS

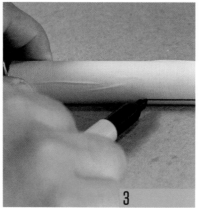

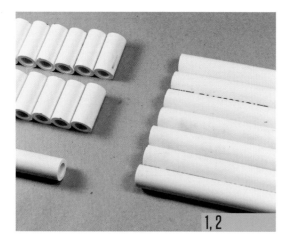

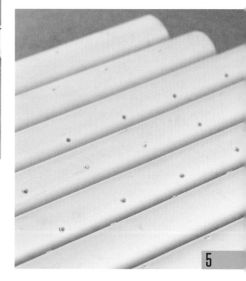

1 — Okay, size. How big do you want your showerhead to be? After measuring my shower, I decided to make mine about 15" wide by 12" long (38 × 30.5 cm)—the dimensions I use in these steps. Although I recommend staying within the size outlined in this project, you can actually make your shower-head as large as you like. Keep in mind that if you have low water pressure and you make a large showerhead, you may not be able to deliver enough water for a satisfying rainfall effect .

2 — Cut seven 12" (30.5 cm) pieces, twelve 1¾" (4.5 cm) pieces, and one 4" (10 cm) piece of pipe. The 1¾" (4.5 cm) pieces are width segments for connecting the fittings, and the 12" (305 mm) pieces are the length segments that produce the spray. The 4" (10 cm) piece will provide the main inlet into the showerhead.

3 — Apply a strip of masking tape along the length of one of the 12" (30.5 cm) pipes. Lay it on a flat surface. Slide a marker along the surface to make a long, straight line down the length of the tape.

4 — Make a mark on the line every 1" (2.5 cm). Drill a ¹/₁₆" (1.6 mm) hole on each mark.

5 — When the holes are drilled in one pipe, remove the tape and apply it to the next 12" (30.5 cm) pipe, making sure that the line is straight, length-wise. Use the tape as a template to drill the next pipe. Repeat this step until all seven pipes are done. If the tape rips, make another one.

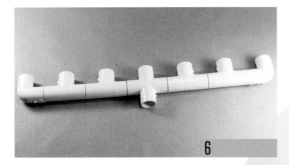

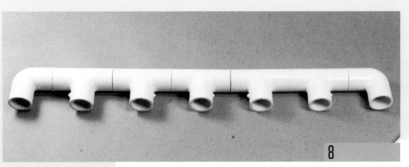

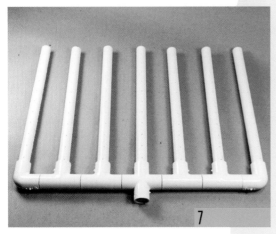

6 _ Now it's time to dry assemble every-thing for testing. Select four tees, two elbows, and a cross member. Use six of the short connector pieces to connect them as shown in the photo.

7 _ Insert one of the drilled pipes into each opening on the connectors.

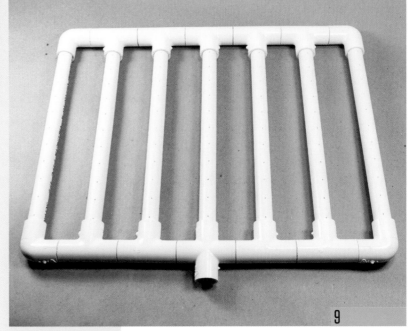

8 _ Connect the remaining five tees and two elbows with six more connector pieces as shown.

9 _ Stick the connectors onto the free ends of the drilled pipes, and rotate all of the pipes so that the holes face downward.

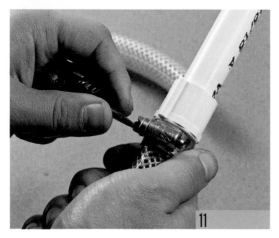

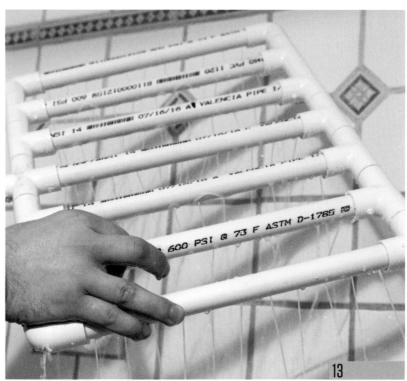

10_Take the 4" (10 cm)-long piece of PVC pipe, and stick the slip to MIP adapter on the end.

11_Force one end of the vinyl tubing over the threads on the male PVC adapter. Heating the vinyl tubing in some hot water or with a hair dryer beforehand will make it easier to slide it over the threads. Once the tubing end is fully over the adapter threads, secure it with a pipe clamp. Insert the 4" (10 cm) piece into the remaining opening of the cross.

12_If you haven't already, remove the showerhead on your shower. Slide a pipe clamp over the vinyl tubing, then slide the tubing over the pipe coming out of the wall. Make sure it slides over about 1 inch (2.5 cm), then secure it with the pipe clamp.

13_Test the showerhead. Slowly and gradually turn the water on. Be ready to turn it off in a hurry if something goes wrong. If you want to change the design, detach it from the shower, modify as necessary, and retest. If some of the nozzles aren't spraying or are spraying at strange angles, clean them out with the drill bit again, as PVC shavings can sometimes clog them.

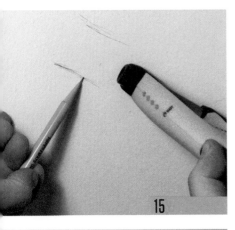

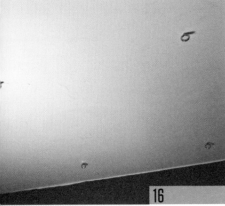

14 — If you're satisfied with how the showerhead is working, remove it, leaving the slip-to-MIP adapter attached to the vinyl tubing. Take all the PVC pieces apart, thoroughly dry the ends and fittings, and glue them together. Take extra care to align the holes downward when you're gluing. Don't glue on the adapter fitting yet, in case you need to make some adjustments later.

15 — When the glue has dried, the showerhead can be hung from the ceiling. First, use a studfinder to figure out where the ceiling joists are above your shower. Mark them with a pencil.

16 — Install the eye screws into the joists. For this design, I decided to hang the showerhead from four individual chains.

17 — Decide how low you want your showerhead to hang, add 4 inches (10 cm), and separate the chain links at that length by using a set of pliers. Here, I have four 24" (61 cm) lengths of chain, but your length will likely be different, depending on your preference and ceiling height. It's a good idea to buy more chain than you need, just in case!

18 — Wrap the chain around a segment of the showerhead and secure the end link around another link. Repeat for the other lengths of chain.

19 — Attach the free end of each chain segment to the eye screws you installed in the ceiling earlier. If necessary, move or shorten the chains so that the showerhead hangs level.

20 — Reattach the vinyl tubing to the threaded end of the showerhead pipe, test it again, and if all is well, glue the showerhead to the adapter fitting. Enjoy your new luxurious rainfall shower!

LAMPS AND LIGHTING

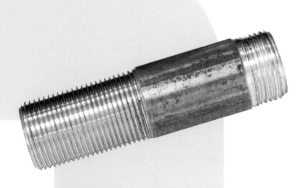

Need a bit more light in your life? The next few projects introduce methods for building romantic candelabras, rustic industrial desk lamps, and even a modern LED ceiling lamp. After starting with these three, you'll come up with your own bright ideas in no time!

CANDLEHOLDER

Projects don't get much better than this: An elegant candleholder that will add a romantic touch to any dinner for two and will look great on every table.

—

This candleholder is easy enough for beginners to tackle and goes together so quickly you can make one for every housewarming. Don't forget to clean the pipe fittings (see page 12) before you get started.

TOOLS

GROOVE-JOINT PLIERS (TWO PAIRS)

SCISSORS (OPTIONAL)

MASKING TAPE (OPTIONAL)

MATERIALS

ONE 1" (25 MM) FLOOR FLANGE

ONE 1" (25 MM) CLOSE NIPPLE

ONE 1" × ½" (25 × 15 MM) REDUCING COUPLER

NINE ½" (15 MM) CLOSE NIPPLES

THREE ½" (15 MM) TEES

THREE ½" (15 MM) 90-DEGREE ELBOWS

ONE ½" × 3" (15 × 76 MM) NIPPLE

FOUR ¾" × ½" (20 × 15 MM) REDUCING COUPLER

FOUR 12" (30.5 CM) TAPER CANDLES

INSTRUCTIONS

1_ Screw the 1" (25 mm) close nipple into the floor flange. Take the 1" × ½" (25 × 15 mm) reducing coupler and spin it onto the close nipple. Use pliers to tighten the assembly. This will be the heavy base of the candleholder.

2_ Select one of the tees and screw in a close nipple. Repeat with the other two tees. The three tees will start the three arms that branch off the main trunk of the candleholder.

3_ Screw the three tees together end to end. Screw the assembly into the base. Tighten the tees so that they form a Y shape when viewed from the top.

4_ Line up the three 90-degree elbows. Screw a close nipple into one end of each.

6

5

7

8

5＿Screw the elbows into the midsections of the tees, making sure that the free ends point up.

6＿Screw close nipples into three of the four ¾" × ½" (20 × 15 mm) reducing couplers. Screw the ½" × 3" (15 × 76 mm) nipple into the last one.

7＿Insert the three reducer and close nipple assemblies into the 90-degree elbows. Tighten them. Twist the reducer and the ½" × 3" (15 × 76 mm) pipe-nipple assembly onto the top tee.

8＿Insert the candles. If your candles are a bit loose in the reducing couplers, simply cut long strips of tape about ½" to ¾" (12 to 19 mm) wide and wrap them around the base of the candles. Twist the candle into the coupler.

DESK LAMP

Tired of seeing the same style of desk lamp in every lighting store? Looking for something unique? Then build your own modern industrial-style desk lamp! The instructions here are for one style, but the process is the important part. Feel free to mix, match, or substitute pipe lengths and fittings to create your own unique design.

TOOLS

WIRE STRIPPERS

**GROOVE-JOINT PLIERS
(TWO PAIRS)**

TWEEZERS (OPTIONAL)

SCREWDRIVER

MATERIALS

**ONE 5" (12.5 CM) CLAMP LIGHT
WITH GUARD**

**ONE ½" (15 MM) FPT TO ¾" (20 MM)
MPT BLACK PIPE BUSHING**

**ONE 1" (25 MM) TO ¾" (20 MM)
BLACK PIPE REDUCING COUPLER**

**ONE ½" (15 MM) BLACK PIPE
CLOSE NIPPLE**

**FOUR ½" (15 MM) BLACK PIPE
90-DEGREE ELBOWS**

**FOUR ½" × 6" (15 MM × 15 CM)
BLACK PIPE NIPPLES**

TWO ½" (15 MM) BLACK PIPE TEES

**ONE ½" × 12" (15 MM × 30.5 CM)
BLACK PIPE NIPPLE**

**TWO ½" × 3" (15 MM × 7.5 CM)
BLACK PIPE NIPPLES**

**ONE ½" (15 MM) STRAIN RELIEF
FITTING**

**TWO ½" (15 MM) BLACK PIPE
END CAPS**

ONE LIGHT-DUTY LAMP PLUG END

ONE EDISON STYLE LIGHTBULB

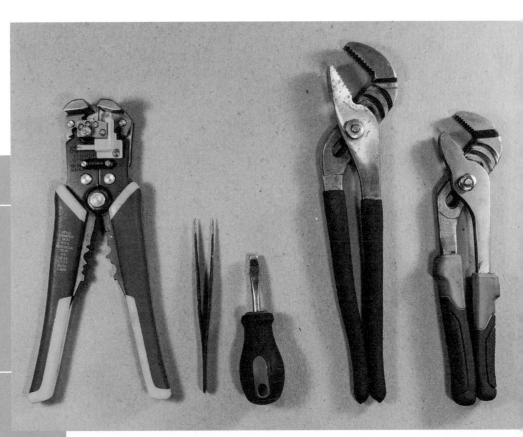

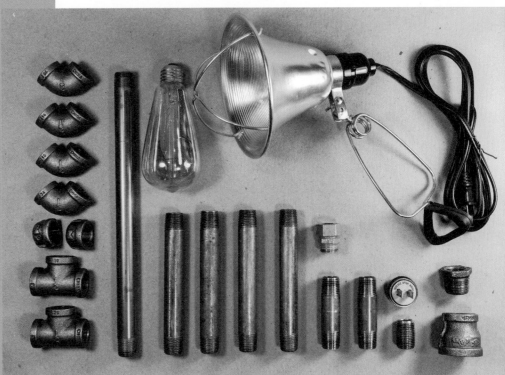

INSTRUCTIONS

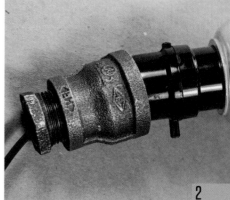

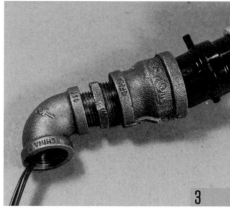

1__ Start with an act of destruction! Remove the clamp from the heat lamp. Using the wire strippers, cut the plug off the end of the cord and throw it away. We'll wire on a new plug at the end of the project. Now would also be a good time to remove any labels or stickers that may be attached to the lamp shroud.

2__ Thread the FPT to MPT coupler into the reducing coupler. Push the lamp cord through the larger end of the newly assembled piece, and pull it all the way through so that the lamp is right up against it.

3__ Twist together the close nipple and a 90-degree elbow, then push the end of the cord through the close nipple and pull it all the way through the 90-degree elbow. Twist the close nipple into the top of the FPT to MPT coupler.

4

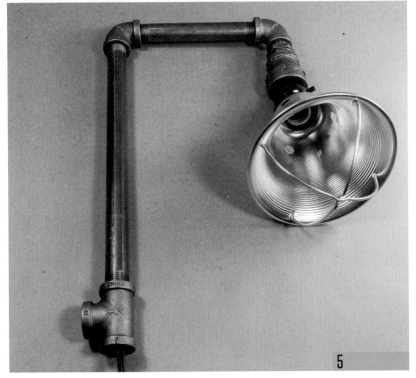

5

6

6 _ Pull the lamp cord tight once more for good measure, then thread it through the strain relief fitting and screw it into the tee. The strain relief fitting has a rubber ring inside that protects the lamp cord from the sharp threads of the tee fitting.

4 _ Screw a 6" (15 cm) pipe nipple into a 90-degree elbow, then run the end of the cord though the pipe nipple and out the elbow. Twist the pipe nipple into the elbow of the already assembled pieces, and tighten it until both elbows are pointing in the same direction. The assembled piece should look like a wide U shape. Pull the lamp cord tight so that the lamp stays close to the couplers.

5 _ Put a tee on the end of the 12" (30.5 cm) pipe nipple as shown, then run the end of the lamp cord through the pipe nipple and out of the opposite end of the tee. Screw the pipe nipple into the elbow, tightening it so that the tee points away from the lamp, and then push the end of the lamp cord back up through the middle of the tee.

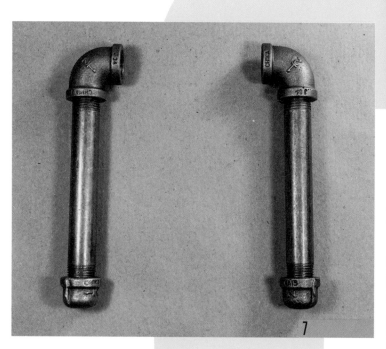

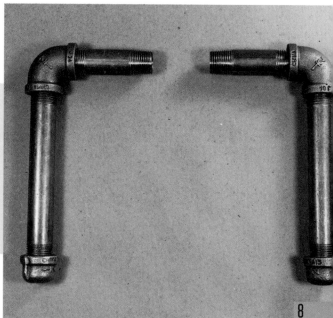

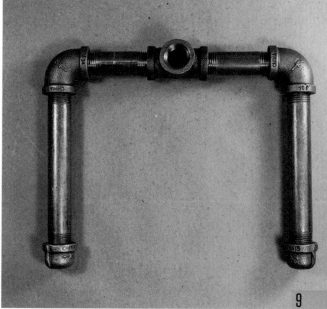

7_ Set the lamp assembly aside, and start building the base. Take two 6" (15 cm) pipe nipples and screw one end cap onto each of them. Screw the two 90-degree elbows onto the other sides of the pipe nipples.

8_ Insert a 3" (7.5 cm) pipe nipple into each of the 90-degree elbows. Tighten them.

9_ Insert the 3" (7.5 cm) pipe nipples into either side of a tee. Tighten them until both 6" (15 cm) pipes are pointing in the same direction and the middle section of the tee is perpendicular to them (it should point upward).

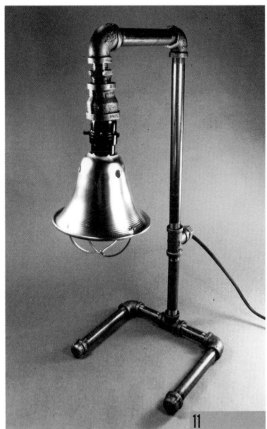

10 _ Screw the last 6" (15 cm) pipe nipple into the tee, and then screw the other end into the tee on the lamp assembly. Tighten until the 6" (15 cm) pipe nipples are pointing in the same direction as the rest of the lamp assembly.

11 _ Separate the wires at the end of the lamp cord, and strip about ½" (13 mm) of insulation from both of them. Follow the instructions provided on the plug end's packaging to wire the plug. If you have never wired a plug before, it's a good idea to seek help from someone who has, or at least have an expert double-check your work before plugging it in!

12 _ Insert a bulb in the lamp, plug it in and test it! Put the lamp on a desk where everyone who visits will be jealous that it's yours.

MODERN CEILING LAMP

Are you looking to update that old chandelier hanging in your dining room? Thanks to LED (light emitting diode) technology, lights run a lot cooler than they used to, which opens up PVC as a great material for building fixtures! I designed this ultramodern ceiling lamp with my own dining room in mind, but these techniques can be applied to other designs that use T8 size LED bulbs.

The wiring here is for 120 volt LED bulbs (they don't need a ballast). Don't try to use it with normal fluorescent bulbs! The 1/8 IP male threaded loop and 1/8 IP washer, lock washer, and nut are lamp parts carried by most lighting supply stores.

TOOLS

DIAGONAL CUTTERS	**SPRAY PAINT**
FILE	**MASKING TAPE**
WIRE STRIPPER	**DRILL**
PVC CUTTER (OR A HACKSAW)	**⅜" (4.5 MM) DRILL BIT**
ELECTRICAL TAPE	**PLIERS**
PVC PRIMER AND GLUE *(and gloves for protection)*	**PHILLIPS SCREWDRIVER**

MATERIALS

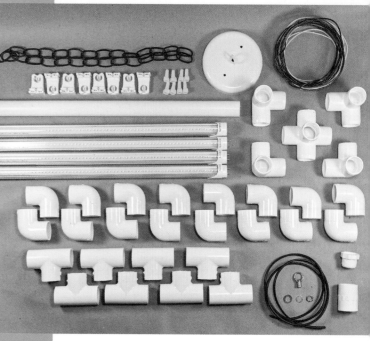

EIGHT NONSHUNTED TURN-TYPE "TOMBSTONE" T8 LED BULB SOCKETS

EIGHT 1" (25 MM) PVC TEES

FOUR 24" (61 CM) 120V 10W T8 LED TUBE BULBS

APPROXIMATELY 6' (1.8 M) OF 14-GAUGE SOLID COPPER INSULATED WIRE (WHITE)

APPROXIMATELY 6' (1.8 M) OF 14- GAUGE SOLID COPPER INSULATED WIRE (BLACK)

9' (2.7 M) OF 1" (25 MM) PVC PIPE

SIXTEEN 1" (25 MM) PVC ELBOWS

FOUR 1" (25 MM) PVC 3-WAY ELBOWS (FURNITURE GRADE)

ONE 1" (25 MM) PVC 5-WAY FITTING (FURNITURE GRADE)

SIX TO EIGHT YELLOW WIRE CONNECTORS

ONE 1" (25 MM) PVC THREADED COUPLER

ONE 1" (25 MM) PVC THREADED PLUG

2' TO 4' (61 CM TO 1.22 M) OF LAMP CORD

1/8 IPS MALE THREADED LOOP

1/8 IPS WASHER, LOCK WASHER, AND NUT

2' TO 4' (61 CM TO 1.22 M) ACCESSORY CHAIN

LAMP CANOPY

INSTRUCTIONS

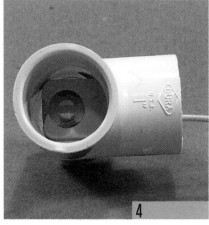

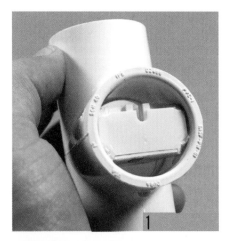

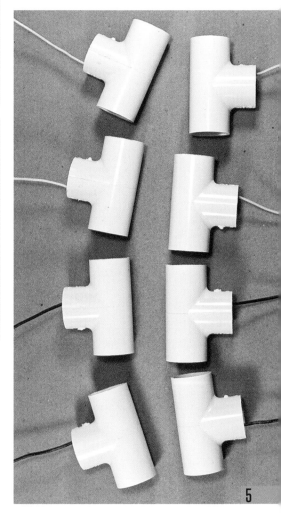

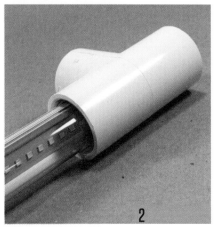

MODIFY AND INSTALL THE SOCKETS

1_Select one of the T8 lamp sockets. Use a pair of diagonal cutters (or a file) to trim the corners of the base as shown so that it fits snugly inside the middle of a tee. It should be pushed in as far as possible, but still be capable of being removed.

2_With the socket inserted into the tee, test that the LED tube will slide into the tee and twist-lock into place. Remove it and the socket from the tee.

3_Cut approximately 12" (30.5 cm) of white wire. Strip about ½" (13 mm) of insulation off each end and insert one end into the connector on the socket.

4_Insert the socket into the tee, pushing it in all the way.

5_Repeat steps 1 through 4 for each socket and each tee. Use white wire for three more and black wire for the other four.

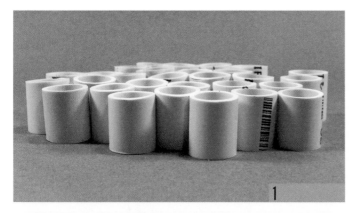

1

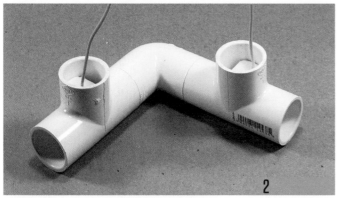

2

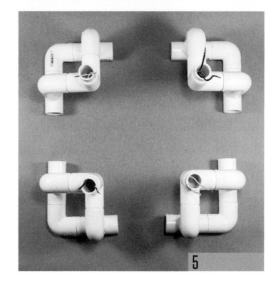

3

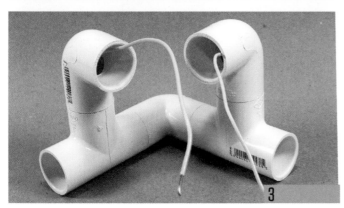

4

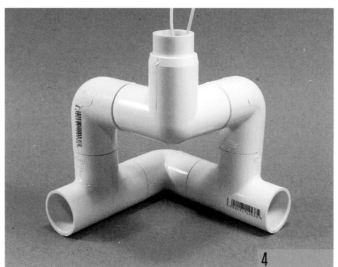

5

BUILD THE CORNERS

1__ Cut twenty-nine 1½" (4 cm) segments of 1" (25 mm) pipe. You'll use these pieces for joining all of the fittings.

2__ Select two of the tees with matching wire colors and use two joining segments to connect them with an elbow fitting as shown. Make sure you don't connect the sides where the LED tubes will be inserted!

3__ Insert joining segments over the wires and into the middle of the tees. Add two elbows.

4__ Insert joining segments into all the openings on a three-way elbow. Thread the two wires into two of the openings and out of the third, then connect it to the two elbows.

5__ Repeat steps 2 through 4 three more times to build the other three corners.

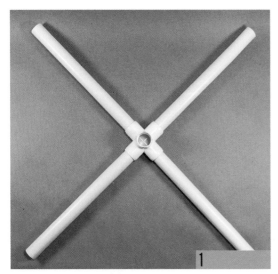

1

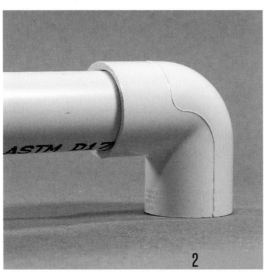

2

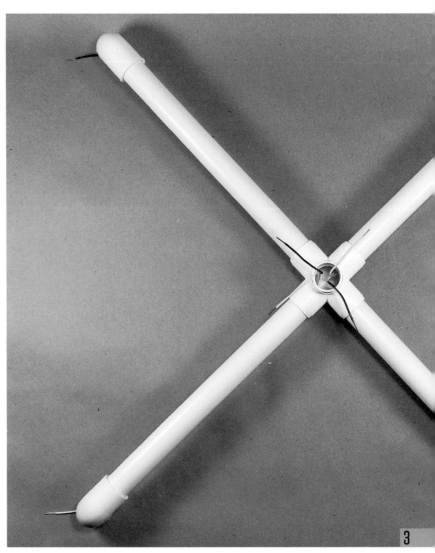

3

3 _ Cut two 24" (61 cm) pieces of white wire and two 24" (61 cm) pieces of black wire. Strip about ½" (13 mm) of insulation off each end. Thread these into the pipes with matching colors opposite each other diagonally.

PUT IT ALL TOGETHER

1 _ Cut four 14¾" (37 cm) sections of 1" (25 mm) PVC pipe. Insert them into the four bottom openings on the 5-way fitting.

2 _ Put an elbow on the end of each pipe segment, with the openings pointing downward.

4

6

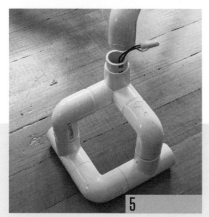

5

7

6 — Carefully push the wire connections into the joining segments. Connect the corners to the elbows.

4 — Orient each corner assembly near an elbow with matching wire color.

5 — Using wire connectors, connect the three matching wire colors at each corner, then wrap electrical tape around them.

7 — If you want to paint your lamp, now is the time! Glue all the vertical pipes into their fittings (the horizontal ones shouldn't need glue). Use masking tape to mask the inside of the fittings. Be sure to paint the top of the threaded plug as well, but mask its threads first!

WIRE IT UP

1_ Thread the lamp cord through the center of the male threaded loop, leaving about 4" (10 cm) of cord sticking out.

2_ Glue the remaining joining segment into the top of the 5-way fitting. Glue on the threaded coupler.

3_ Drill a ⅜" (9 mm) hole in the center of the threaded plug. Insert the loop's threads through the hole so the loop is inside the plug, then secure the loop with a washer, lockwasher, and nut. Tie a knot in the cord to keep it from pulling through the loop.

4_ Separate the end of the lamp cord, and strip about ½" (13 mm) of insulation from each. Use a wire connector to connect one of the wires to the white wires, and another wire connector to connect the other wire to the black wires. Don't forget to wrap electrical tape around them when done!

INSERTING BULBS

Inserting the bulbs might require twisting and flexing the pipe a bit. Twist and flex gently! The trickiness of getting the bulbs in is worth your time—because they're LED, they could last for over twenty years!

5 — Twist the threaded plug tight into the coupler while holding the wire to make sure it doesn't spin and twist.

6 — Attach the fixture chain to the 1/8 IPS male threaded loop, removing links as necessary. Thread the lamp cord through the chain, then trim the wire, leaving it 6" (15 cm) longer than the chain. Separate the end of the lamp cord and strip ½" (13 mm) of insulation from each wire.

7 — Turn off the power supply to the ceiling fixture at the electrical panel. Remove the existing ceiling fixture. Use a circuit tester to check that the power is off.

Attach the chain to the canopy loop and thread the wire through the hole. Wire the lamp cord into the ceiling fixture. Attach the canopy to the fixture box. Turn the circuit breaker on and give your fancy new LED ceiling lamp a try!

FURNITURE

We all need furniture, but why settle for overpriced one-size-fits-all solutions from a big-box store? In the following six projects, you'll learn how to build stylish and practical furnishings for every room of the house! Whether you're relaxing on a bed you made yourself, or displaying your bike with a wall-mount bike rack, there's a feeling of satisfaction that these projects deliver that you can't buy at a store.

FOUR-POSTER BED FRAME

This industrial-style bed, made with black-metal pipe, can be adapted to either an elegant four-poster, or a simple postless bed. Either way, the sturdy bed frame design provides a comfortable place to sleep that can easily be disassembled if you need to move it. While these instructions are for a queen-sized mattress, you can easily change the lengths of the pipes to fit whatever mattress you have.

TOOLS

SMALL TRIANGULAR FILE
(OPTIONAL)

PIPE WRENCH/LARGE PLIERS

TAPE MEASURE

PENCIL

HANDSAW

DRILL (WITH BIT FOR
SCREWS)

MATERIALS

SIX 1½" × 1" (40 × 25 MM)
REDUCING COUPLERS

SIX 1" × 12" (25 MM × 30.5 CM)
PIPE NIPPLES

TWELVE 1" (25 MM) TEE FIT-
TINGS

FIVE 1" (25 MM) CLOSE NIPPLES

SIX 1" × 10" (25 MM × 25.5 CM)
PIPE NIPPLES

FOUR 1" × ¾" (25 × 20 MM)
REDUCING COUPLERS

SIX 1" × 36" (25 MM × 91.5 CM)
PIPES

FIVE 1" (25 MM) COUPLERS

TWO 1" × 6" (25 MM × 15 CM)
PIPE NIPPLES

SIX 1" × 18" (25 MM × 45.5 CM)
PIPES

THREE 1" (25 MM) UNIONS

TWO 1" × 24" (25 MM × 61 CM)
PIPES

TWO 1" (25 MM) 90-DEGREE
ELBOW FITTINGS

FOUR ¾" × 36" (20 MM × 91.5 CM)
PIPES

FOUR ¾" × ½" (20 × 15 MM)
REDUCING COUPLERS

FOUR ½" (15 MM) 90-DEGREE
ELBOW WITH SIDE OUTLET
FITTINGS

EIGHT ½" × 18" (15 MM × 45.5 CM)
PIPES

FOUR ½" × 36" (15 MM × 91.5 CM)
PIPES

FOUR ½" (15 MM) COUPLERS

TWO ½" × 6" (15 MM × 15 CM)
PIPE NIPPLES

FOUR ½" (15 MM) UNIONS

TWO ½" × 24" (15 MM × 61 CM)
PIPES

FIFTEEN 1" × 4" × 96"
(2.5 CM × 10 CM × 2.4 M) BOARDS

FIFTY-TWO 1¼" (32 MM)
WOOD SCREWS

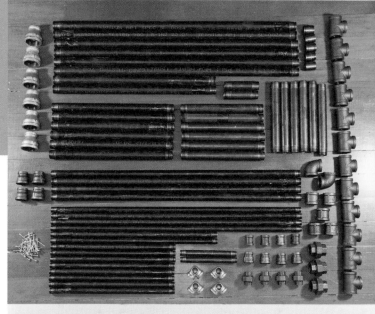

INSTRUCTIONS

MAKE THE BED FRAME

1_Since the threads on the 1" (25 mm) pieces of pipe are so large, they may have chips or defects left over from the manufacturing process. Examine the threads for any potential issues, and if necessary, clean up the threads with a small triangular file. It's not a bad idea to give the ¾" and ½" (20 and 15 mm) pipe ends a good look, too.

2_First, assemble the legs using 1" (25 mm) pipe. Starting from the bottom up, connect a 1½" × 1" (40 × 25 mm) coupler, 12" (30.5 cm) pipe nipple, tee, close nipple, tee, 10" (25.5 cm) pipe nipple, and a 1" × ¾" (25 × 20 mm) coupler. When you're done with the first one, make three more.

3_The 1½" (40 mm) couplers are the feet for the bed. With the feet oriented downward, the bed rails will connect to the lower tees, and the cross members at the head and foot of the bed will connect to the upper tees. Rotate the tees on each leg to reflect which corner they belong to. They should match the photo when you're done.

4_Build the first bed rail using 1" (25 mm) pipe by attaching a 36" (91.5 cm) pipe, a coupler, a 6" (15 cm) pipe nipple, a tee, and a 36" (91.5 cm) pipe together. Repeat for the second rail.

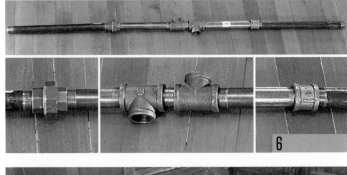

5 — Attach one of the bed rails to the lower tees on two of the legs. Do the same for the other rail and remaining two legs. The tees in the middle of the bed rails should both be pointed inward, matching the upper tees on their respective legs.

6 — To connect the two bed rails, build a midbrace using 1" (25 mm) pipe. Connect an 18" (45.5 cm) pipe, a coupler, a 10" (25.5 cm) pipe nipple, a tee, a close nipple, a tee, a 10" (25.5 cm) pipe nipple, a union, and a 18" (45.5 cm) pipe together, as shown in the photo. Tighten up the midbrace as much as possible, but make sure that the tees in the middle are opposite each other. Leave the union loose.

7 — Attach the midbrace to the middle tees of the bed rails. The tees in the middle of the midbrace should be pointing at the head and foot of the bed. Once both sides of the midbrace are firmly tightened to the bed rails, tighten up the union.

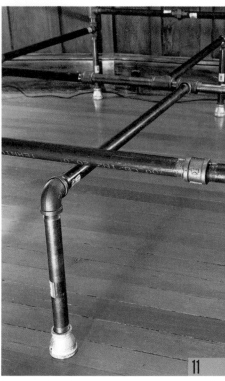

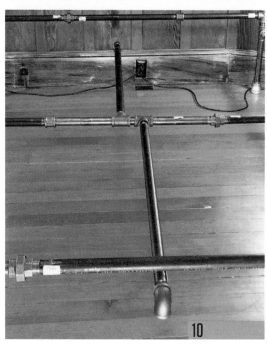

8 __ Assemble a head/foot rail using 1" (25 mm) pipe. Connect an 18" (45.5 cm) pipe, a coupler, a 24" (61 cm) pipe, a union, and a 18" (45.5 cm) pipe, then make another one. Remember to leave the unions loose until the next step.

9 __ Attach the head/foot rails between the upper tees on the legs, then tighten their unions.

10 __ Because the bed is wide, it will need bed-slat supports that screw into the tees in the midbrace. Attach a 1" (25 mm) elbow to the end of a 1" × 36" (25 mm × 91.5 cm) pipe, then screw it into a tee in the midbrace, and do the same for the other tee. The open ends of the elbows should point downward when they're tightened.

11 __ Screw a 1½" × 1" (15 × 25 mm) coupler "foot" onto the end of a 1" × 12" (25 mm × 30.5 cm) pipe nipple, then screw it into one of the elbows. Repeat for the other elbow.

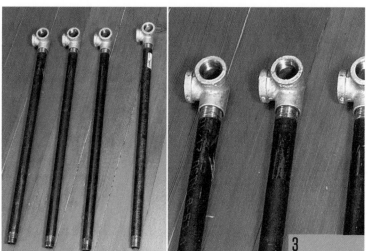

ADD THE POSTS AND CANOPY RAILS

1_If you want simple postless bed, skip straight to the Add the Slats instructions. The following seven steps are decorative, adding the post extensions and upper-canopy rails. Now is also a good time to grab that step stool, as the next steps require working up high.

2_Select four ¾" × 36" (20 mm × 91.5 cm) pipes. Add a ¾" × ½" (20 × 15 mm) coupler to one side of each, then screw them into the couplers at the top of each leg.

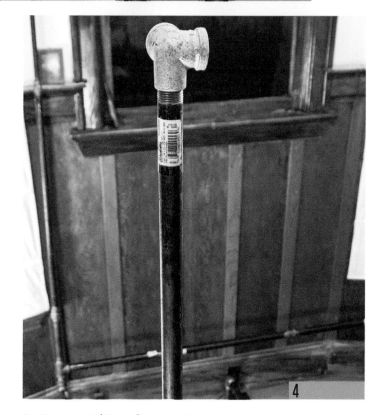

3_Attach a ½" (15 mm) elbow with side outlet to the end of each of four ½" × 18" (15 mm × 45.5 cm) pipes, to create corner fittings.

4_Screw the ½" × 18" (15 mm × 45.5 cm) pipes into the couplers at the top of the legs, tightening them so that the openings in the corner fittings match the direction of the bed rails and head/foot rails.

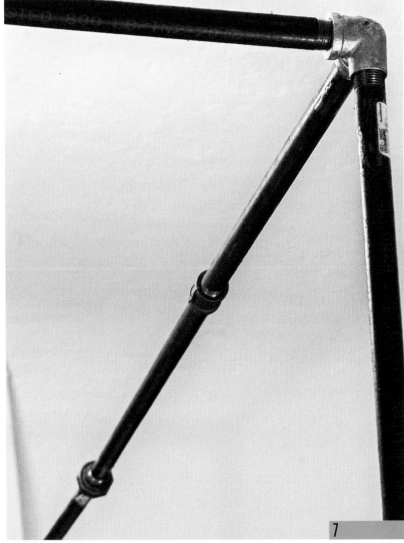

5 Now it's time to add the canopy side rails. Using ½" (15 mm) pipe, connect a 36" (91.5 cm) pipe, a coupler, a 6" (15 cm) pipe nipple, a union, and a 36" (91.5 cm) pipe to make one side rail. Repeat to make another. Leave the unions loose until the next step.

6 Install the side rails between the corner fittings, then tighten the unions.

7 Assemble each of the two canopy head/foot rails with ½" (15 mm) pipe. Connect an 18" (45.5 cm) pipe, a union, a 24" (61 cm) pipe, a coupler, and an 18" (45.5 cm) pipe. As in step 6, install the rails between the corner fittings, and tighten the unions.

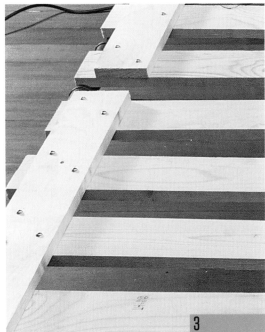

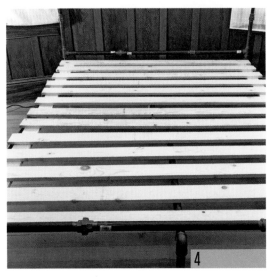

ADD THE SLATS

1_ With the frame of the bed done, it's time to add the bed slats that support the mattress. Take 13 of the boards, and cut each them down to the width of the bed frame so that the ends are supported by the side rails (about 65½" [1.66 m] long).

2_ Equally space the cut boards across the bed frame. To keep the boards from shifting, they need to be connected to boards that run perpendicular and sit along the side rails. We'll cut those in the next step.

3_ Cut two boards to 35" (89 cm), and two more to 40" (101.5 cm). Lay the boards across the bed slats on either side, just inside the bed rails. Secure them with two wood screws where they cross each slat.

4_ Flip the bed slats over so that the newly attached side-rail boards are on the bottom, add a queen-size mattress, and you're done! Enjoy your new industrial-chic bed!

TABLE

Whether you're a college student with your first apartment, a hobbyist in need of a work surface, or you simply need a little extra table space, here is a table you can make yourself. It's a cinch to put together, and if you need to store it, it can easily be broken down into its component parts. I'm showing mine with an unfinished top. You could top yours with a polished board, a stone slab, or mosaic tiles.

TOOLS

GROOVE-JOINT PLIERS (TWO PAIRS)

DRILL WITH PHILLIPS BIT

HANDSAW FOR WOOD (OPTIONAL)

TAPE MEASURE (OPTIONAL)

MATERIALS

**FOUR 1" × ¾" (25 × 20 MM)
REDUCING COUPLERS**

**EIGHT ¾" × 12" (20 MM × 30.5 CM)
PIPE NIPPLES**

SIX ¾" (20 MM) TEES

**FOUR ¾" × 8" (20 MM × 20.5 CM)
PIPE NIPPLES**

FOUR ¾" (20 MM) FLOOR FLANGES

**ONE ¾" × 36" (20 MM × 91.5 CM)
PIPE NIPPLE**

**ONE LARGE BOARD, APPROXIMATELY
29" × 45" × ½" (73.5 × 114.5 × 1.3 CM)**

SIXTEEN ½" (13 MM) WOOD SCREWS

INSTRUCTIONS

1_ Start by assembling one of the table legs. Select one of the 12" (30.5 cm) pipe nipples and screw it into a reducing coupler.

2_ Screw one of the tees onto the opposite end of the pipe nipple.

3_ Select another 12" (30.5 cm) pipe nipple and screw it into the top of the tee.

4_ Finish the top of the leg by adding a floor flange. The flange will mount to the underside of the table surface once the frame is completed.

5_ Follow steps 1 through 4 three more times to assemble the other table legs. Make sure that all the connections are tight.

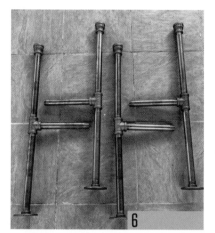

9＿Cut your tabletop board to the desired dimensions. Lay the tabletop face down on the floor. Place the table frame flange-side down on top of it.

10＿Position the frame exactly where you want it. Use the drill to drive four screws through each of the floor flanges. Flip your table right-side up and enjoy!

6＿Screw the four 8" (20.5 cm) long pipe nipples into the tees on each leg.

7＿Connect two of the legs using a tee between the 8" (20.5 cm) long pipe nipples. Do the same for the other pair of legs.

8＿Connect the two pairs of legs, using the 36" (91.5 cm)-long pipe nipple. Tighten the connection so that all of the floor flanges are pointing in the same direction. The table frame is now complete.

CHAIR

This wood and iron-pipe chair requires only a handful of tools to build. It's the perfect sturdy companion to the iron-pipe table. But then again, it's handsome enough to stand on its own as well. There's a definite sense of satisfaction in sitting in a chair that you built yourself. Use a staple gun to attach foam padding and frabric or leather for an upholstered finish.

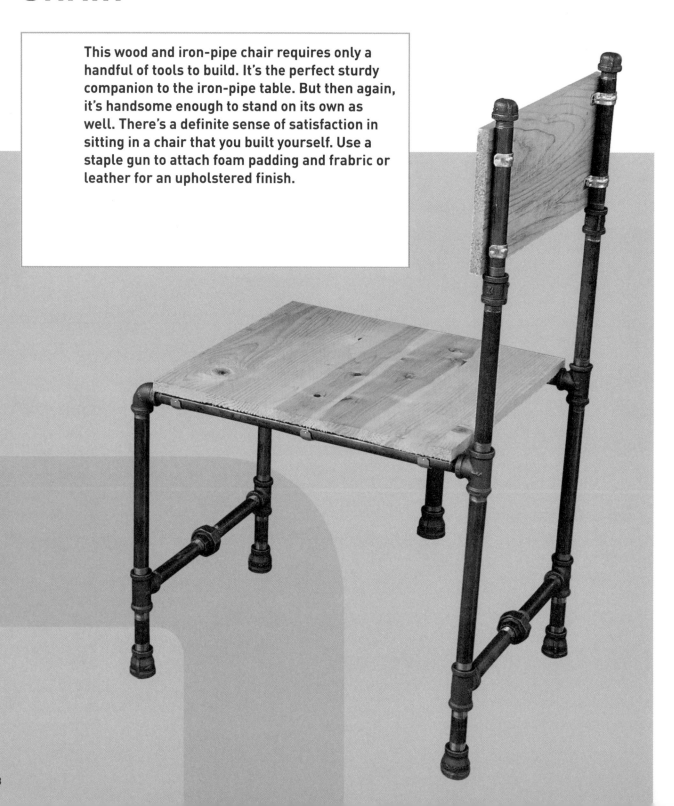

TOOLS

GROOVE-JOINT PLIERS (TWO PAIRS)

DRILL WITH PHILLIPS BIT

SAW FOR WOOD (OPTIONAL)

TAPE MEASURE (OPTIONAL)

PENCIL (OPTIONAL)

MATERIALS

**FOUR ¾" × ½" (20 × 15 MM)
REDUCING COUPLERS**

**FOUR ½" × 3" (15 MM × 7.6 CM)
PIPE NIPPLES**

SIX ½" (15 MM) TEES

**FOUR ½" × 10" (15 MM × 25.5 CM)
PIPE NIPPLES**

TWO ½" (15 MM) 90-DEGREE ELBOWS

**TWO ½" × 18" (15 MM × 45.5 CM)
PIPE NIPPLES**

**FOUR ½" × 6" (15 MM × 15.5 CM)
PIPE NIPPLES**

TWO ½" (15 MM) UNIONS

**FOUR ½" × 8" (15 MM × 20.5 CM)
PIPE NIPPLES**

TWO ½" (15 MM) COUPLERS

TWO ½" (15 MM) CAPS

**ONE 17" × 16" × ½" (43 × 40.5 × 1.3 CM)
WOODEN BOARD**

**ONE 7" × 16" × ½" (18 × 40.5 × 1.3 CM)
WOODEN BOARD**

**TEN ¾" (20 MM) EMT
ONE-HOLE STRAPS**

TEN ½" (13 MM) WOOD SCREWS

INSTRUCTIONS

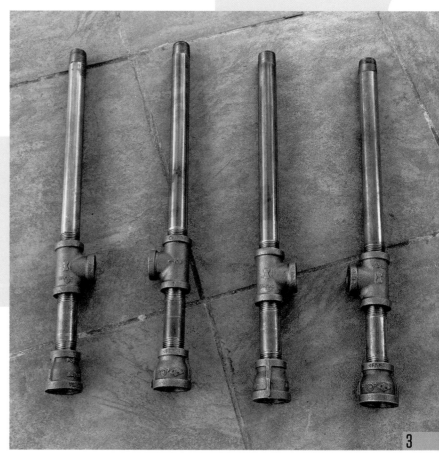

1_ Thread one 3" (7.5 cm) pipe nipple into one reducing coupler. Repeat to form the start to the chair's four legs.

2_ Select four of the tees and thread them onto the ends of the pipe nipples.

3_ Thread the four 10" (25.5 cm) pipe nipples into the tops of the tees. You now have four identical chair legs.

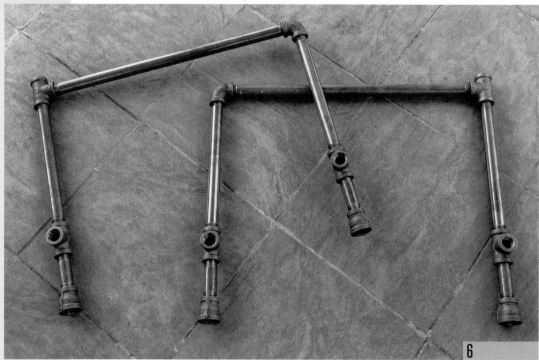

4_ Take two of the legs and screw a 90-degree elbow onto the end of each. These will be the chair's front legs. Tighten everything so that the elbows are pointing away from you and the midsections of the tees are pointing toward each other.

5_ Take the other two chair legs and screw the remaining two tees onto the end of each. These are the two back legs of the chair, so tighten everything up with the lower tee midsections pointing toward each other, and the upper tee midsections pointing toward you.

6_ Attach one of the back legs to its corresponding front leg using one of the 18" (45.5 cm) pipe nipples between the elbow and the tee. It might be a bit awkward, spinning these two pieces together, so be patient! Repeat this step again for the other two legs with another 18" (45.5 cm) pipe nipple.

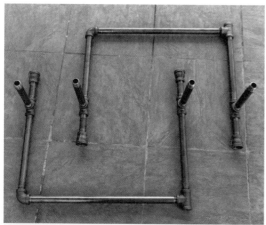

7_ Now you can connect the four legs with crossbars. Select the four 6" (15 cm) pipe nipples. Screw each one into the lower tees in each leg.

8_ Select the two unions and screw one side of each onto the 6" (15 cm) pipe nipples on the left half of the chair. Position the right half of the chair in place and screw the other side of the unions to the 6" (15 cm) pipe nipples. Tighten everything up. All four legs are connected!

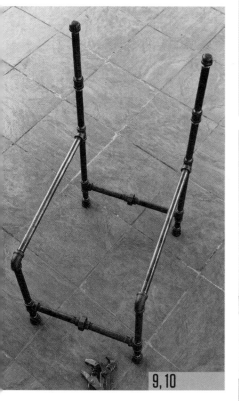

9 _ Now focus on the chair's back. Select two of the 8" (20.5 cm) pipe nipples. Screw them into the tops of the tees on the rear legs.

10 _ Screw a cap to one end and a coupler to the other end of the remaining 8" (20.5 cm) pipe nipples. Twist them onto the pipe nipples on the back of the chair. All the pipe work is done!

11 _ Prepare the boards for the sitting surface and backrest. Break out your handsaw, circular saw, or table saw and cut the boards to size. The sitting surface should be 17" × 16" (43 × 40.5 cm), and the back rest 7" × 16" (18 × 40.5 cm). If you were lucky enough to have the hardware store cut your boards to size for you, you can skip this step!

12 _ With the boards cut, we need to attach them to the chair frame. If the frame still seems a bit wobbly, this step should resolve it. Flip the chair forward, and place the sitting surface on top of the 18" (45.5 cm) pipes. Center it, then use the drill, screws, and one-hole straps to attach the board to the pipe, as shown.

13 _ Using four of the one-hole straps and screws, attach the backrest to the chair, as in step 12, resting the board between the couplers and caps on the upper half of the chair back.

WALL-MOUNT SHELF

Same old, same old! So many shelf units available at an affordable price look so similar. Want something special? Make one instead! This three-tier shelf will perfectly complement your new iron-pipe table and chairs. It's great for holding souvenirs or mementos, and the pipes running through on each side work as perfect bookends.

TOOLS

MARKER/PENCIL

DRILL

⅞" (22.5 MM) SPADE BIT

PHILLIPS HEAD BIT FOR SCREWS

MATERIALS

FOUR ½" × 6" (15 MM × 15 CM)
PIPE NIPPLES

FOUR ½" (15 MM) 90 DEGREE ELBOWS

FOUR ½" × 3" (15 MM × 7.5 CM)
PIPE NIPPLES

FOUR ½" (15 MM) FLANGES

THREE SHELF BOARDS (RECOMMENDED
¾" × 10" × 24" [2 × 25.5 × 61 CM])

FOUR ½" × 8" (15 MM × 20 CM)
PIPE NIPPLES

TWELVE ½" (15 MM) COUPLERS

SIX ½" (15 MM) CLOSE NIPPLES

SIXTEEN 1½" (38 MM)
WALL-MOUNTING SCREWS

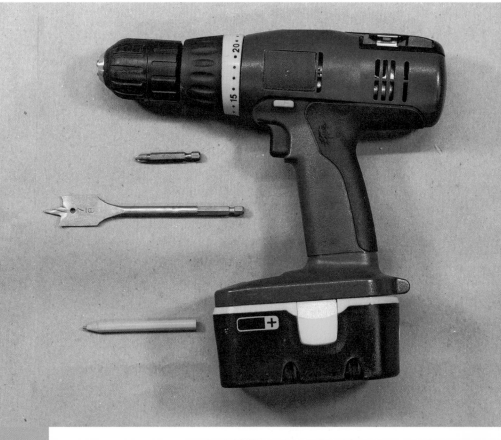

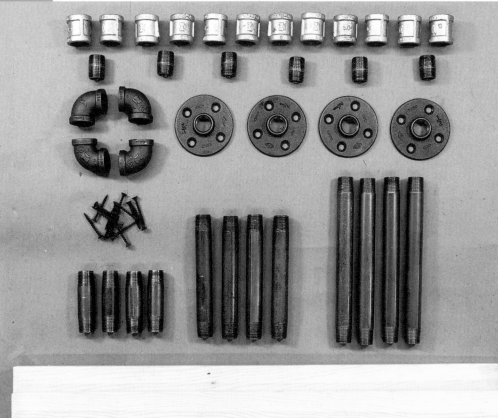

INSTRUCTIONS

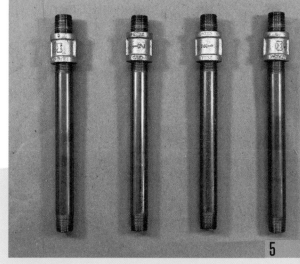

1__ Assemble one of the wall braces by screwing a 6" (15 cm) pipe nipple into an elbow. Screw the elbow onto a 3" (7.5 cm) pipe nipple, then screw a flange onto the nipple.

2__ Place one of the shelf boards on a flat surface on its long edge. Hold the assembled wall brace on the flat surface, sliding it up to the end of the shelf board. Use the position of the nipple's end to mark where a hole should be made in the board. Repeat on the other end of the board.

3__ Stack the three shelf boards on top of each other, with the marked board on top, and align the edges. *Optional: Clamp them together to prevent movement while drilling.* Using a drill with the spade bit, drill holes at each of the marks, going all the way through the top board, middle board, and bottom board. This ensures that all three boards will line up when the shelf is assembled.

4__ Assemble three more of the wall braces, and tighten them up as much as possible.

5__ Set out the 8" (20.5 cm) nipples. Screw a coupler onto one end of each, then a close nipple into the coupler. We'll call these the shelf spacers.

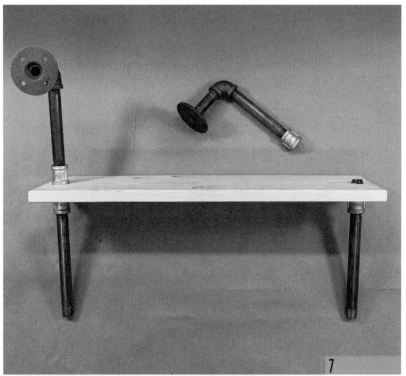

6 — Take two wall braces, and screw couplers onto the ends of the 6" (15 cm) nipples.

7 — Insert the close nipple ends of two shelf spacers through the holes in a board. Screw the exposed threads into the couplers on the wall braces. If no threads are exposed, it's okay to unscrew the close nipple a little bit so that they are. The board should now be supported between the couplers.

8 — Screw two more couplers onto the bottom of the shelf spacers on the bottom of the board.

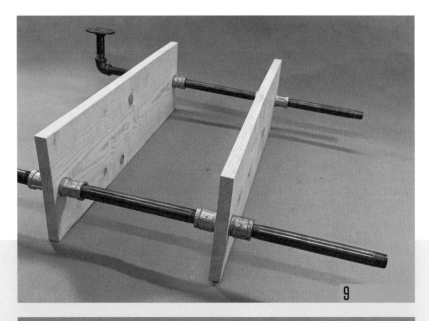

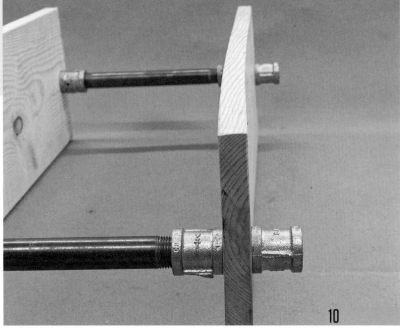

9 — Repeat steps 7 and 8 with a second board, screwing the close nipple threads into the shelf spacer couplers beneath the first board.

10 — Screw two couplers and two close nipples into the bottom of the shelf spacers. Place the third board over them and screw on the remaining two couplers.

11 — Take the last two wall braces and screw them into the couplers. The shelf is done and ready to be mounted to the wall!

12_ Hold the shelf up to the wall where you want to mount it (with a supporting stud behind it). Screw one screw through one of the top flanges, leaving it slightly loose so that the shelf hangs from it. Due to the weight of this unit, at least one side must be attached to a stud. Use heavy-duty wall anchors for the other side if it doesn't align with studs. (Note that if you use an anchor, you may need to predrill and install the anchor behind the flange before you attach the shelf to the wall.)

13_ Rotate the other side of the shelf upward so that the shelves are level, and screw a second screw into the other top flange.

14_ If the shelf looks good as is, screw in the remaining screws through the top and bottom flange holes to finish mounting the shelf!

WINE RACK

Are you someone who likes to save wine for a special occasion but lacks a dusty old wine cellar for storage? Don't just hide it in a cupboard—display the bottles in style by building a one-of-a-kind wine rack! The instructions here are for a six-bottle version, but the design can be scaled up or down to accommodate however many bottles you'd like—for yourself or to give as a gift.

TOOLS

MEASURING TAPE

PENCIL

PVC CUTTER OR HACKSAW

PVC PRIMER AND CEMENT

SANDPAPER (OPTIONAL)

SPRAY PAINT (OPTIONAL)

MATERIALS

3' × 1" (91.5 CM × 25 MM) PVC PIPE

SIX 1" (25 MM) PVC TEES

TWO 1" (25 MM) PVC ELBOWS

INSTRUCTIONS

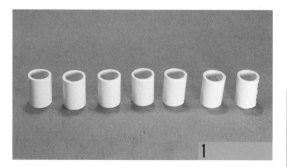

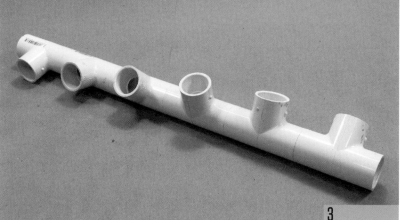

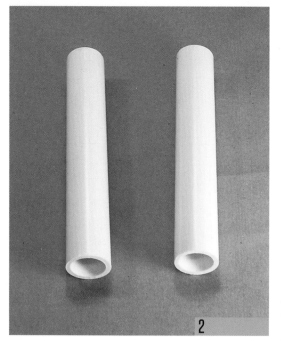

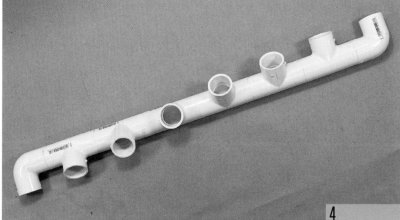

1 — Cut seven 1¾" (4.5 cm) segments of pipe.

2 — Cut two 8" (20.5 cm) segments of pipe.

3 — Attach all the tees, end to end, with the 1¾" (4.5 cm) segments of pipe. Rotate each tee so that it points in a different direction than the previous. I arranged mine so that the line of bottles would transition from one side of the holder to the other.

4 — Use the last two 1¾" (4.5 cm) segments of pipe to add elbows to the end, pointing them in opposite directions as shown.

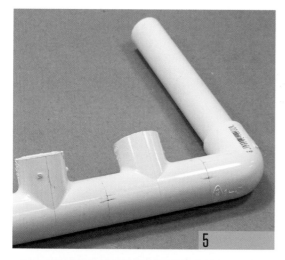

5

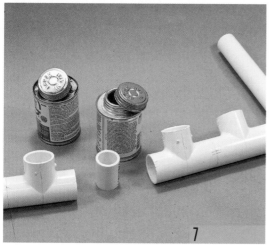

7

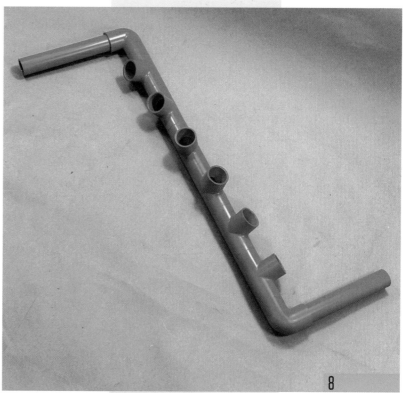

8

5 — Insert an 8" (20.5 cm) pipe segment into each of the elbows.

6 — Test the holder by inserting a bottle into each tee and tweaking the tee arrangement as necessary. When you're satisfied, mark the position of each tee and take them apart.

7 — Reassemble each connection using PVC primer and cement to make sure that the pieces don't slip.

8 — After letting the glue dry, give it a good surface sanding and decorative coat of paint. (See page 10 for painting tips). Your wine rack is ready to use!

WALL-MOUNT BIKE RACK

Hang your bike on the wall with the rest of your artwork with this simple, inexpensive bike rack. Not only is it functional, it's easy to make and easy to install. It also doubles as a place to store your helmet, gloves, and other bike accessories!

TOOLS

TAPE MEASURE

HACKSAW

PERMANENT MARKER

CARPENTER'S SQUARE

COPING SAW

⅛" (3 MM) DRILL BIT

DRILL

METAL FILE OR SANDPAPER (OPTIONAL)

MATERIALS

ONE 6" (15 CM) PVC PIPE
(Often called a "riser" pipe. Typically comes in 2 foot [61 cm] sections)

ONE PIECE OF 2 × 4 (38 × 89 MM) PINE
(at least 6" [15 cm] long)

THREE 3" (76 MM) SCREWS

FOUR ¾" (19 MM) SCREWS

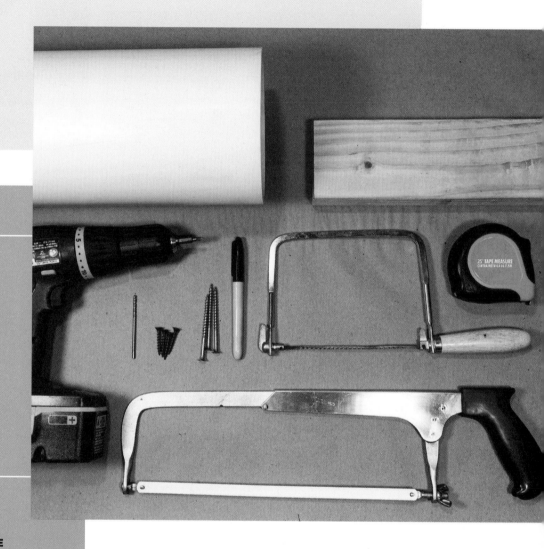

INSTRUCTIONS

1 _ To make sure your bike will hang at the correct distance from the wall, measure the width of the handlebars from outside edge to outside edge. Take that number, divide it by two, then add about 3" (7.5 cm). The resulting number is the length that the 6" (15 cm) pipe should measure. In my case, that length is 12" (30.5 cm).

2 _ Before cutting the pipe, draw a line all the way around the pipe at the length you want to cut it. Having a line to follow when you cut makes it easier to keep your cut straight. Using the hacksaw, start cutting into the pipe, making a shallow cut and rotating the pipe to continue along the line. When you've made a shallow cut along the entire line, start cutting all the way through the pipe, using the shallow cut to guide the saw.

3 _ Return to your bike and roughly measure the diameter of the top tube of the frame. In my case, it was about 1⅛" (28 mm).

4 _ Find a circular object that's just slightly larger in diameter than the top tube measurement. I used the cap from a can of spray solvent. In the next steps, we'll be using this object as a guide to mark the cuts we'll be making. If you can't find a circular object the right size, you can always cut a circular template out of paper.

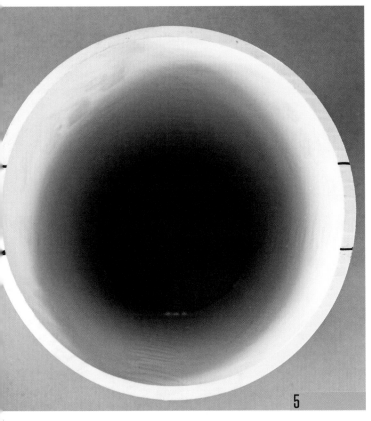

5 Hold the circular template to the flat end of the pipe, and mark around its widest section. Then move the template directly opposite the mark you just made (but on the same face), and trace around its widest point again. Your two pairs of marks should resemble the picture here.

6 Pick one of the pairs of marks, and draw two 2" (5 cm) lines along the side of the pipe, perpendicular to the end. It's helpful to have a carpenter's square to assist you here. Once this section is cut out, it will be the part of the rack that the bike frame first slides into.

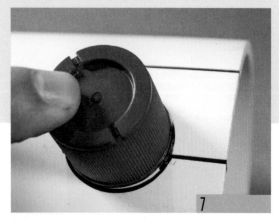

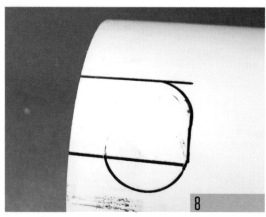

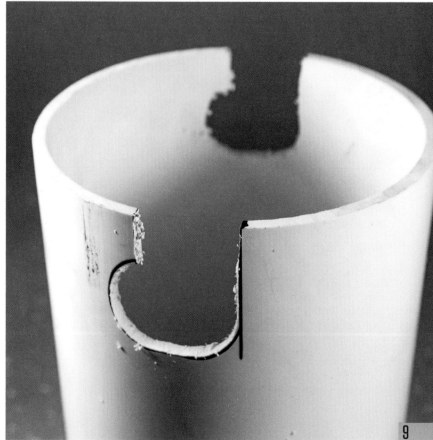

7_ To make sure the bike doesn't slide out of the rack, we need to give it a place to drop into. Place your circular template on the lower line so that half of it is below and half of it is above, with the line stopping at the edge of the template. Trace around it. Remove the template, then connect the top line to the bottom line. This L shape will form the channel that the bike's frame rests in.

8_ Follow the same steps you used to make the first set of marks to mark the other side of the pipe. Make sure that both L's are pointing downward.

9_ Using a coping saw (or jigsaw or rotary tool), cut out the shape you just marked on either side of the pipe. For a more polished appearance, use files or sandpaper to smooth the cuts.

10

11

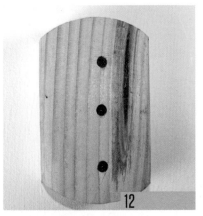

12

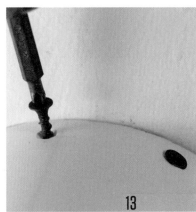

13

10 — Put the uncut end of the pipe on top of the board. Trace around the inside of the pipe. Using the coping saw again, cut along the traced lines so that the wood will just slip inside the pipe.

11 — Once the wood fits, orient it so that it runs perpendicular to the cuts across the end of the pipe. This will ensure that the pipe is well supported by the wood when the bike is hanging from it. On either end of the wood, drill two holes through the pipe and into the wood. After the wood is secured to the wall, these holes will get screws that secure the pipe to the wood.

12 — Find a stud in your wall, and use the 3" (7.6 cm)-long screws to secure the wood to the wall where you want your bike to hang. I used three screws for good measure. Make sure that the length of the wood is running vertically.

13 — Slide the PVC pipe over the wood, lining up the previously drilled holes with the holes in the wood, and secure it with four screws. Your bike rack is finished! Now tell your friends exactly how you made it, since they'll probably want to make their own, too.

Ready for some epic outdoor fun? This next section contains some of the largest and most technically challenging projects in the book, but they're also some of the most rewarding. Whether you're looking to win the neighborhood water-fight, enjoy a yurt in your backyard, or just relax in your garden to the sound of a shishi-odoshi, turn the pages and start building!

OUTDOORS

SHISHI-ODOSHI

Maybe you've never heard of a *shishi-odoshi*, but you've probably seen one. This style of Japanese fountain was originally used to keep animals away from crops and gardens— gently, with the sound of water. The name *shishi-odoshi* translates as "deer scarer."

—

A traditional *shishi-odoshi* is made of bamboo, but this durable PVC version will look great in your garden while keeping the local wildlife at bay!

TOOLS

MEASURING TAPE	DRILL
PENCIL	5/16" (8 MM) DRILL BIT
UTILITY KNIFE	TWO SETS OF PLIERS
HALF-ROUND FILE	DIAGONAL CUTTERS
PVC PRIMER AND GLUE *(and gloves for protection)*	1" (25 MM) HOLE SAW
RUBBER MALLET	DUCT TAPE
SANDPAPER	FLATHEAD SCREWDRIVER

MATERIALS

80" (2.03 M) OF 1½" (40 MM) PVC PIPE

TWO 1½" (40 MM) PVC TEES

TWO 1½" (40 MM) PVC ELBOWS

ONE 1" (25 MM) PVC PLUG

ONE 1½" (38 MM) RUBBER O-RING

ONE 1½" (40 MM) PVC CROSS

TWO 1½" (40 MM) PVC END CAPS

TWO 1" (2.5 CM) LONG × 5/16" (8 MM) STAINLESS STEEL BOLTS

FOUR 5/16" (8 MM) STAINLESS STEEL WASHERS

TWO 5/16" (8 MM) STAINLESS STEEL LOCK WASHERS

TWO 5/16" (8 MM) STAINLESS STEEL NUTS

LARGE WATERTIGHT BASIN OR TROUGH *(24" [61 cm] in diameter recommended)*

APPROXIMATELY 2' (61 CM) SQUARE OF ½" (1.3 CM) 19-GAUGE HARDWARE CLOTH *(or similar)*

12" (30.5 CM) OF ¾" (20 MM) PVC PIPE

SPRAY PAINT (OPTIONAL)

APPROXIMATELY 5' (1.5 M) × OF ½" (13 MM) ID VINYL TUBING

TWO STAINLESS STEEL 5/16" TO 7/8" (8 × 22 MM) HOSE CLAMPS

ONE ½" (15 MM) 90-DEGREE HOSE BARB FITTING

ONE EXTRA-SMALL FOUNTAIN PUMP (RATED FOR 1½' TO 2' (45.7 TO 61 CM) PUMPING HEIGHT

FOUR MEDIUM ZIP TIES

SMOOTH ROCKS (ENOUGH TO COVER THE HARDWARE CLOTH)

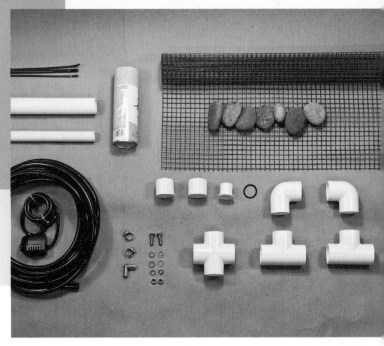

INSTRUCTIONS

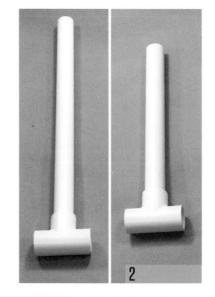

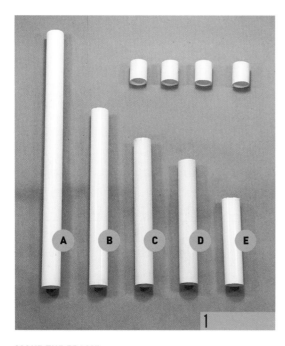

MAKE THE FRAME

1_ Cut the following lengths of 1 1/2" (40 mm) pipe:

One 24" (61 cm)	(A)
One 16" (40.5 cm)	(B)
One 13" (33 cm)	(C)
One 11" (28 cm)	(D)
One 7½" (19 cm)	(E)

Four 2" (5 cm) joining pipes

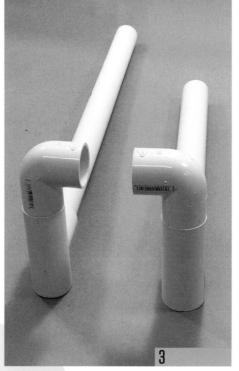

2_ Insert pipe A into the middle of a tee, and do the same for pipe B.

3_ Use a joining pipe to add an elbow to one side of each tee.

4_ Rotate the elbows so they face each other. Join them with pipe E, but don't glue anything yet!

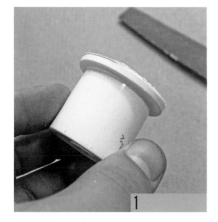

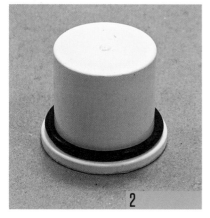

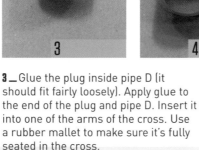

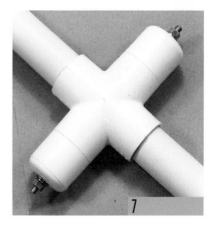

BUILD THE CROSS PIPE

1_Take the plug, and use a knife or file to scrape the flashing off the outer rim of the flange portion. You should be able to insert and remove if from the cross without too much force.

2_Slide the rubber O-ring over the plug until it's against the flange.

3_Glue the plug inside pipe D (it should fit fairly loosely). Apply glue to the end of the plug and pipe D. Insert it into one of the arms of the cross. Use a rubber mallet to make sure it's fully seated in the cross.

4_Glue pipe C into the opposite side of the cross.

5_Sand or file the lettering off the outside of both end caps. Drill a $5/16$" (8 mm) hole in the center of each.

6_Put a washer on each bolt. Insert the bolts from the inside of the caps so that the threads stick out. Add another washer, then a lock washer, and then, finally, a nut. Tighten everything.

7_Glue the remaining joiner pipes into the caps. Glue them into the cross, opposite each other.

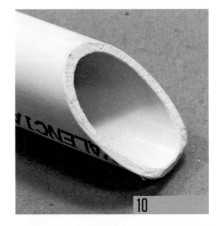

10

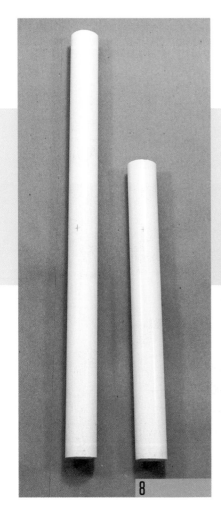

8

11

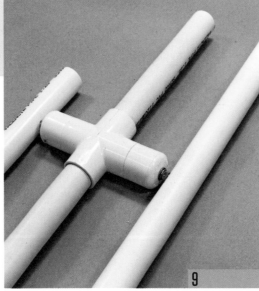

9

10 _ Use a hacksaw to make a shallow angle cut across the end of pipe D as shown. This will help it to catch and fill with water.

11 _ Reassemble the frame with the cross in the middle. Make sure that the cross is still able to rotate freely!

8 _ Remove pipes A and B. Make a mark 12" (30.5 cm) from the end on each.

9 _ Drill a ⁵/₁₆" (8 mm) hole in both pipes (not all the way through!). Insert the bolts that protrude from the cross end caps. They should be able to rotate freely without any binding. If the bolts go in but won't spin freely, try running the drill bit in and out of the hole a few more times to enlarge it a bit.

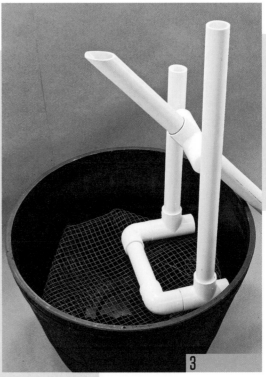

3_ Place the *shishi-odoshi* on the platform and let pipe C rest on the edge. If you don't want the pipe to strike the edge of the basin, place a large rock under it that it will stick up over the edge of the basin. Test the configuration by pouring water into pipe D. Once enough water is in the pipe, it should rotate to empty itself, then spin back to its original position. I raised mine a bit and flipped the base for a little extra room.

BUILD THE BASE AND FIT THE WATER SPOUT

1_ Set out the large basin. Decide where you want the *shishi-odoshi* to sit inside it, so that pipe C rests on the edge, and pipe D is able to pour water into the basin. For my *shishi-odoshi*, I decided to have it sit a little lower than halfway inside, right up against the edge.

2_ Cut the hardware cloth to a size that fits inside the basin at the required level, forming a platform. The *shishi-odoshi* will sit on this platform, with the pump under the hardware cloth so that it gets plenty of water.

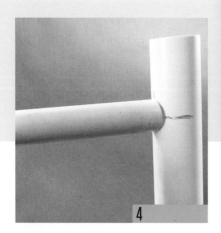

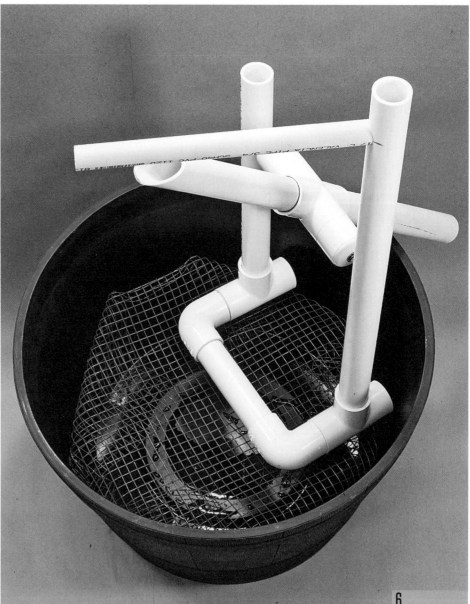

4＿Make a pencil mark about 1½" to 2½" (3.8 to 6.5 cm) from the top of pipe A. Place the ¾" (20 mm) pipe on the mark, and rotate it around pipe A until it points directly at the end of pipe D. Mark its position. This will be where the water spout comes out.

5＿Remove pipe A. Drill into the mark on the pipe using a 1" (25 mm) hole-saw in a drill. Try to insert the ¾" (20 mm) pipe. File the hole with a half-round file if necessary. It should be a tight fit!

6＿Once the ¾" (20 mm) pipe fits, reinsert pipe A in the frame. Make sure that everything lines up as expected. Don't worry about the length of the ¾" (20 mm) pipe yet; we'll cut it down in a later step. For now, remove it and set it aside.

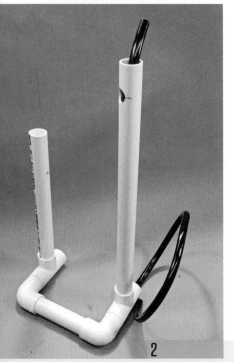

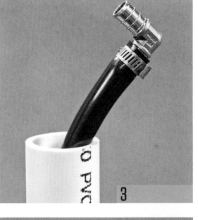

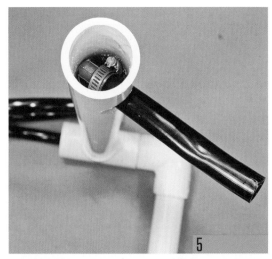

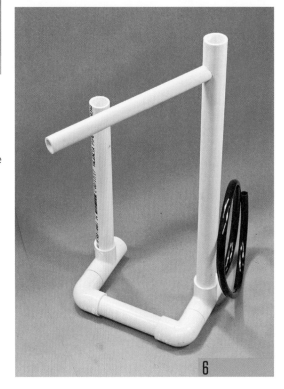

3_ Put a hose clamp over the tubing. Insert the brass 90-degree hose barb fitting. Tighten the hose clamp around it.

4_ Slide the other hose clamp over the open end of the barb fitting and push the fitting down inside pipe A so that the free end is at the level of the hole.

PLUMBING, PAINTING, AND FINISHING

1_ Cut a 5" (12.5 cm) piece of vinyl tubing. Set it aside.

2_ Run the long piece of vinyl tubing through the open end of the tee and out the top of pipe A.

5_ Insert the short piece of vinyl tubing into the hole and over the end of the hose barb. Secure it with another hose clamp.

6_ Slide the ¾" (20 mm) pipe over the exposed vinyl tubing and into pipe A.

7_Attach the fountain pump to the other end of the vinyl tubing. Submerge it in water, plug it in, and turn it on. If your pump's flow rate can be adjusted, do so while observing how the water comes out of the end of the pipe. Pick the setting that seems right and make a good guess as to how long the pipe should be in order for the stream to hit and fill the end of pipe D. Best to err on the side of being too long—you can always cut it shorter but you can't cut it longer!

Use a bit of duct tape to hold pipes A and B together during this step since they aren't glued yet. Turn off the pump, remove and cut the ¾" (20 mm) pipe, then reinsert it and test it again. Once you're satisfied, turn the pump off and move to the next step.

8_Mark all the fittings in relation to each other to make it easy to reassemble. Remove the tubing. Disassemble the frame for gluing. Apply glue to the ends and reassemble all the pieces except the water spout and pipe E. If you want to add a bit of color, now is the time to paint.

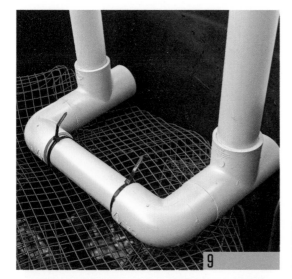

9_When you've reassembled everything and run the tubing back inside pipe A, put the pump under the hardware cloth platform and attach the tubing. Put the *shishi-odoshi* on the platform and zip tie the base to it.

10_ Arrange rocks on top of the hardware cloth to hide the base and the pump underneath. Fill the basin with water. If needed, brace the hardware cloth by placing rocks or bricks underneath it. I used upside down flowerpots.

11_ Plug the pump in, turn it on, and put your soothing new water feature where it can be appreciated (and keep deer away)!

YURT

In the steppes of central Asia, many nomadic peoples dwell in portable, round, tent-like structures called yurts. Yurts typically have a wooden lattice frame, but for this light-duty adaptation, we use PVC and plastic sheeting. This yurt is not built to withstand heavy winds and rainstorms, but can be enjoyed for weekend camping trips, or as a relaxing space to hang out in during a summer rain. It's simple to make—especially if you have a friend handy to help—and it's designed to be taken apart and rebuilt as often as you want.

TOOLS

TAPE MEASURE

PVC CUTTER OR HACKSAW

RUBBER MALLET

DRILL

¼" (6 MM) DRILL BIT

PERMANENT MARKER

PVC PRIMER AND GLUE
(and gloves for protection)

SCISSORS

MATERIALS

TWENTY-TWO 10' (3 M) LONG 1" (25 MM) PVC PIPES

FORTY-EIGHT 1" (25 MM) PVC TEES

TWENTY-FOUR 1" (25 MM) PVC 45-DEGREE ELBOWS

SIXTY-FOUR 2" (5 CM)-LONG ¼"-20 (6 MM) BOLTS

SIXTY-FOUR ¼"-20 (6 MM) WING NUTS

100' × 10' (30. 38 M × 3 M) OF 4 MIL CLEAR PLASTIC SHEETING
(UV-rated, preferably)

INSTRUCTIONS

2_Make the central ring. Use 8 tees, 8 elbows, and 16 E pieces to make the ring as shown. This will serve as the hub for the roof's spokes.

3_Insert an A piece into each of the tees on the ring you just made—eight in all. This will give you a good idea of how big the yurt will be when it's done.

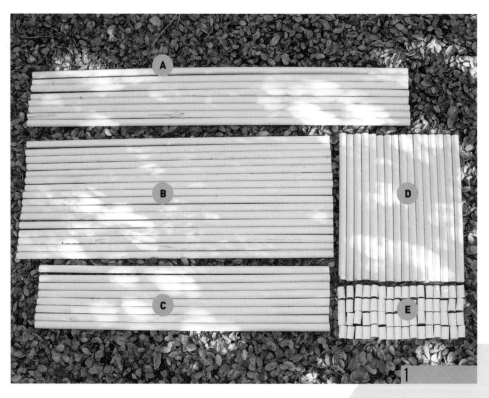

MAKE THE ROOF

1_Using the PVC cutter or hacksaw, cut the pipes into the following pieces:

Eight 72" (1.8 m)	(A)
Sixteen 25" (63.5 cm)	(B)
Eight 51½" (1.3 m)	(C)
Sixteen 57" (1.45 m)	(D)
Sixty-four 2" (5 cm)	(E)

4_Make the roof-base pieces. Slide a tee onto a B, add another tee and B, a third tee, an E, an elbow and finally another E to build a roof base piece as shown. Repeat seven more times for a total of eight roof-base pieces. These will connect the A pieces to finish the roof and connect the roof to the walls.

5_Connect the central tee of each roof-base piece to each A piece, keeping the elbows on the right side. When all are connected, prop up the central ring with a chair, and connect the ends of each roof-base piece together. A rubber mallet will make this a lot easier!

ADD THE WALLS

1_ Make the wall-base pieces. Put a tee on either end of each C piece. On the right side of each, add an E piece, followed by an elbow and another E piece. Repeat seven more times for eight wall-base pieces, in total.

2_ Insert a D piece into each of the tees in the wall bases. Insert the other end of each D piece into a corresponding roof base piece, raising the roof. This step is a little awkward, but a rubber mallet makes the job easier. I recommend completing the four sides opposite each other first, then filling in the gaps between them. When all of the vertical pieces are in, connect the wall bases together as in step 5, on page 105. When all of the pieces are together, use the rubber mallet to tap the pipes and fittings into place. In the next steps, we'll add bolts and glue, so it's important to have all the pieces aligned just right.

ADD THE BOLTS AND GLUE

1_ Using a ¼" (6 mm) drill bit, drill a hole at each place where the roof base, wall base, and central ring join other pipes and each other. This will make it easier to disassemble the yurt into its major components later, rather than taking apart every single piece. When the holes are drilled, insert a 2" (5 cm) bolt and finish it with a wing nut.

2_ For each of the joints that did not get a bolt, use the permanent marker to make a mark across the two pieces. For each marked joint, disassemble and glue the pieces together, being sure to line up the marks again. Don't forget to glue the central ring as well.

ADD THE ROOF PLASTIC

Have another person help you with the following steps, if you can.

1_To reach the roof and add a plastic cover, you'll need to disassemble the walls. Once the glue from the previous steps has dried for at least 15 minutes, remove any bolts holding the vertical wall pipes (D pieces), and lower the roof to the ground.

2_Roll out the plastic sheeting over the right-hand side of the roof so that it overlaps the center by about 8" (20.5 cm).

3_Tape the plastic into place at the roof's central ring and on the roof base.

4_Holding the plastic taut, use the scissors to cut it about 12" (30.5 cm) from the edge of the roof base so that it overhangs the edge.

5_Follow steps 2 to 4 again, but for the left-hand side, overlapping the center again. Run a long piece of tape along the overlapping edge to secure the two pieces together. Don't worry if the plastic sags a bit—we'll tighten it up in a later step. With the roof plastic in place, reassemble the walls with their bolts.

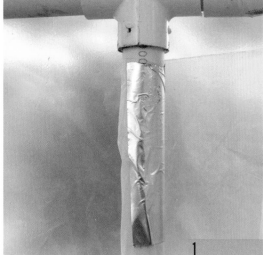

FINISH UP

1＿Don't let your helpful volunteer leave yet! Decide where the entrance will be. Unroll a long section of plastic and wrap the free end around the inside of a pipe bordering the entrance. Secure it with tape.

2＿Unroll the plastic all the way around the walls, securing the top edge with tape on the inside as you go. When you reach the pipe on the opposite side of the entrance, cut it and wrap it around the pipe, securing it with tape.

3＿Trim the bottom edge of the plastic all the way around the yurt, leaving about a 4" (10 cm) border. Wrap the border under the wall bases, pull it tight, and secure it inside with tape.

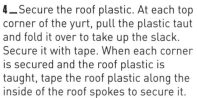

4 _ Secure the roof plastic. At each top corner of the yurt, pull the plastic taut and fold it over to take up the slack. Secure it with tape. When each corner is secured and the roof plastic is taught, tape the roof plastic along the inside of the roof spokes to secure it.

5 _ If you like, use the remaining plastic to add a door flap. Enjoy your yurt!

SUPERPOWERED WATER BLASTER

Those store-bought water guns have all sorts of problems—the tanks are too small, the stream is too weak, and what's the fun in just buying something anyway? Make your own better version! With this water blaster, you will reign supreme over every water fight in your neighborhood. So get building!

TOOLS

DRILL

½" (13 MM) DRILL BIT

¼" (6 MM) DRILL BIT

ADJUSTABLE WRENCH

PLIERS

FILE

SANDPAPER

SCISSORS

GEL INSTANT GLUE

PVC PRIMER AND GLUE (AND GLOVES FOR PROTECTION)

PETROLEUM JELLY

¾" (19 MM) SPADE BIT (OR ¾" [19 MM] HOLE SAW)

FLATHEAD SCREWDRIVER

MATERIALS

¾" (20 MM) PVC PLUG

⅜" ID × ¼" (3 × 6 MM) MIP BRASS HOSE BARB

THIN RUBBER SHEET

DUCT TAPE

TWO 1⅛" (28 MM) RUBBER O-RINGS

APPROXIMATELY 6' (1.83 M) OF ⅜" (9 MM) ID × ½" (13 MM) OD VINYL TUBING

ONE MEDIUM ZIP TIE

24" (61 CM) OF 1" (25 MM) PVC PIPE

1" (25 MM) PVC TEE

4" (10 CM) OF 1" (25 MM) PVC PIPE

1" (25 MM) PVC END CAP

21" (53.5 CM) OF 1¼" (32 MM) PVC PIPE

1¼" (32 MM) PVC TEE

4" (10 CM) OF 1¼" (32 MM) PVC PIPE

1¼" (32 MM) PVC END CAP

1¼" (32 MM) PVC COUPLER

1¼" TO ¾" (32 × 20 MM) PVC THREADED BUSHING

¾" (20 MM) BRASS CLOSE NIPPLE

¾" (20 MM) THREADED PVC CHECK VALVE

¾" (20 MM) MIP TO MALE GARDEN HOSE BRASS ADAPTER

FEMALE GARDEN HOSE TO ¼" OD (6 MM) BRASS SWIVEL ADAPTER

TWO 3" (80 MM) PVC END CAPS

⅜" ID × ½" MIP (9 × 15 MM) BRASS HOSE BARB

24" (61 CM) OF 3" (80 MM) PVC PIPE

5/16" TO ⅞" (7 TO 22 MM) STAINLESS STEEL HOSE CLAMP

SHOULDER STRAP (OPTIONAL)

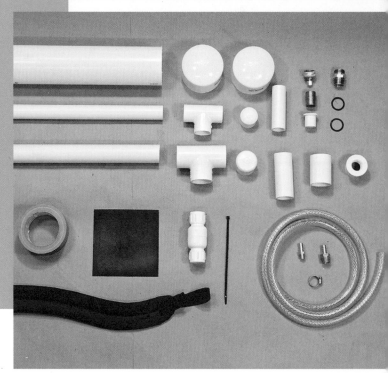

INSTRUCTIONS

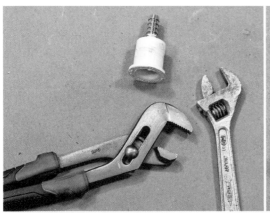

BUILD THE INNER PIPE

1 _ Drill a ½" (13 mm) hole through the center of the plug. Using pliers and a wrench, thread in the MIP hose barb.

2 _ Place the end of the hose barb into the drill chuck and tighten. Use a file and sandpaper to shave down its diameter until it just fits into the end of the 1" (25 mm) PVC pipe.

3 _ Sand the letters off the flat flange face of the plug. On a piece of rubber, trace around the plug flange. Cut a piece of rubber just slightly smaller than your tracing.

4 _ Use sandpaper to rough up a section of the edge of the piece of rubber. Spread a little gel instant glue along a small section of one edge, leaving the rest without glue to form a flap.

5 _ Create a flap by place the piece of rubber glue-side down on the plug's flange. Wait about 5 minutes until it's dry. This flap will act as a one-way valve that will let water in from the hose and out again through the end of the gun.

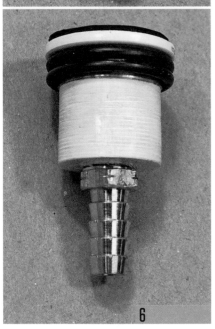

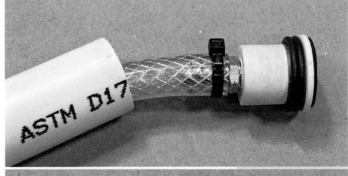

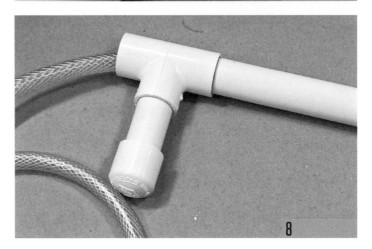

6＿Wrap a narrow, about ⅛" (3 mm), strip of duct tape four times around the plug near the flange. Fit the two O-rings over the duct tape on the flange.

7＿Push the vinyl tube through the 24" × 1" (61 cm × 25 mm) PVC pipe, and slide it over the hose barb. Fasten it with a zip tie and clip off its end. Glue the plug into the end of the pipe, tapping it flush with a rubber mallet.

8＿Make a handle, as shown, using the 4" long 1" (10 cm × 25 mm) PVC pipe, 1" (25 mm) tee, and 1" (25 mm) end cap. Glue it all together on the opposite end of the pipe. Make another handle with 1¼" (32 mm) pieces. Glue it onto the end of the 21" × 1¼" (53.5 cm × 32 mm) PVC pipe.

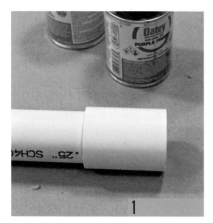

1

2

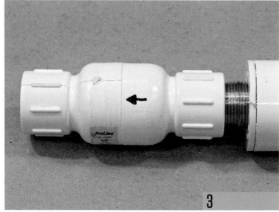

3

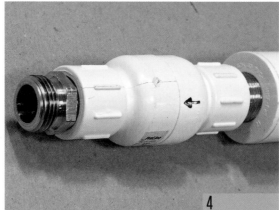

4

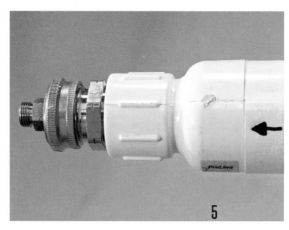

5

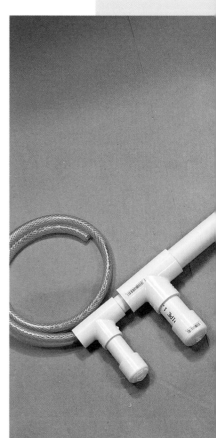

BUILD THE OUTER PIPE

1 _ Glue the 1¼" (32 mm) coupler onto the other end of the 21" (53.5 cm)- long pipe.

2 _ Glue the 1¼" to ¾" (32 × 20 mm) adapter into the end of the coupler.

3 _ Thread the ¾" (20 mm) brass nipple into the adapter. Thread the check valve onto the nipple, with the flow arrow pointing away from the coupler.

4 _ Screw the MIP to male garden hose adapter into the free end of the check valve.

5 _ Attach the female garden-hose to ¼"-OD adapter to the male garden-hose adapter. Remove the small end cap from its end. This finishes the outer pipe. Spread petroleum jelly on the O-rings of the previously constructed inner pipe and push it into the back of the outer pipe.

5

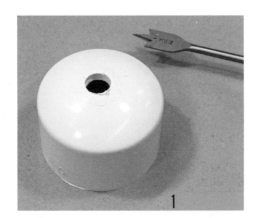

1

3

2

MAKE THE TANK

1＿Drill a hole through the middle of a 3"
(80 mm) end cap with the ¾" (19 mm) spade
bit. Use a wrench to thread the remaining
hose barb into the hole.

2＿Glue the end cap onto the end of the
3" (80 mm) pipe to complete the bottom
of the tank.

3＿Drill a ¼" (6 mm) hole into the
other 3" (80 mm) end cap. This will be
the top of the tank. This hole will allow
air into the tank as water flows into
the tube.

4＿Lubricate the inside of the end
cap with petroleum jelly. Stick it onto
the end of the tank. This will make it
easier to remove when you want to
refill the tank.

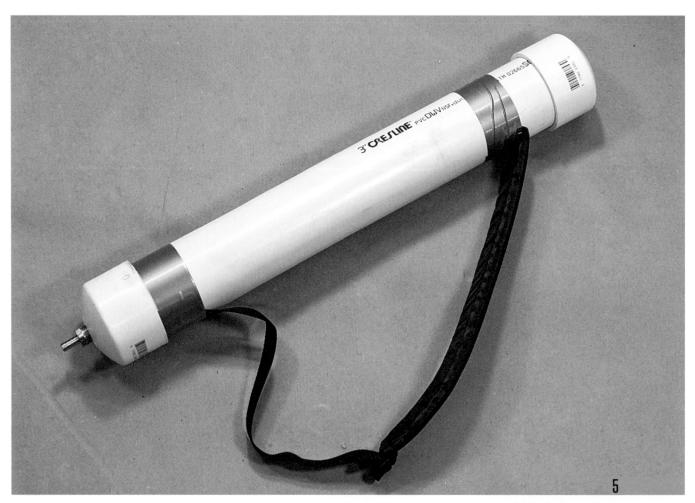

5 _**[OPTIONAL]** Attach a shoulder strap to the pipe with duct tape. I used a piece cut from an old backpack for my strap. Alternatively, you can make a strap out of duct tape folded on itself.

6 _Attach the hose to the hose barb, and secure it with the hose clamp.

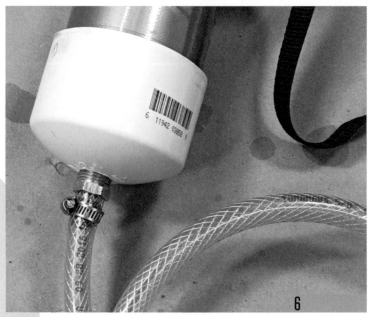

7＿Decorate the pieces. It's a good idea to add orange tape to the end so that other people know it's a toy, but your color scheme can be as wild as you want!

8＿Remove the cap and fill the tank. Put the tank on the blaster and try it out! Pulling out the inner pipe sucks water into the barrel: pushing it back sprays it out! Have a blast!

BICYCLE TRAILER

Do you love riding your bike but get frustrated that you can't take large things with you? Worry no more! With this bicycle trailer, your trips to the hardware or grocery store will be a lot more fun. The quick-connect hitch makes attaching and detaching the trailer super simple.

TOOLS

PVC PIPE CUTTER
(OPTIONAL)

RUBBER MALLET

HACKSAW

PERMANENT MARKER

DRILL

$5/16$" (8 MM) DRILL BIT

PHILLIPS BIT

TWO ADJUSTABLE WRENCHES

PVC PRIMER AND GLUE
(and gloves for protection)

MATERIALS

THREE 10' (3 M) LONG 1"
(25 MM) PVC PIPES

EIGHT 1" (25 MM) PVC ELBOWS

ONE 1" (25 MM) PVC TEE

FOUR 1" (25 MM) PVC CROSSES

2' (61 CM) SLOTTED ANGLE
BRACKET

TEN 2½" (6.5 cm)- LONG $5/16$"
(8 MM) BOLTS

TWENTY $5/16$" (8 MM) FENDER
WASHERS

TEN $5/16$" (8 MM) NYLON
LOCKING NUTS

TWO 16" (40.5 CM) BICYCLE
WHEELS

ONE 90-DEGREE FOUR-HOLE
STRUT BRACKET

TWO #1 CONDUIT HANGERS

TWO 1" (25 MM)- LONG ¼"
(6 MM) BOLTS

FOUR ¼" (6 MM) FENDER
WASHERS

FOUR #10 FINISHING WASHERS

TWO ¼" (6 MM) NYLON
LOCKING NUTS

4" (10 CM) OF ½"-DIAMETER
(13 MM) HEAT-SHRINK TUBING
(OPTIONAL)

TWO ¼" (6 MM) MALE BRASS
QUICK-CONNECT COUPLER
FITTINGS

ONE ½" (13 MM) FENDER
WASHER

ONE ¼" (8 MM) BRASS PIPE CAP

ONE ¼" (8 MM) FEMALE BRASS
QUICK-CONNECT COUPLER
FITTING

6" (15 CM) OF ⅜" (9 MM) 10 × ⅝"
(16 MM) OD VINYL TUBING

ONE ⅜" TO ⅞" (9 TO 22 MM)
PIPE CLAMP

ONE 1" (25 MM) 45-DEGREE
PVC ELBOW

ONE ¾" (19 MM)-THICK WOODEN
BOARD (APPROXIMATELY
33" × 45" [8.4 CM × 1.14 M])

SIX 1¼" (32 MM) EMT
ONE-HOLE STRAPS

SIX ¼" (6 MM) WASHERS

SIX ¾" (19 MM) WOOD SCREWS

EIGHT EYE SCREWS WITH ½"
(13 MM) THREAD (OPTIONAL)

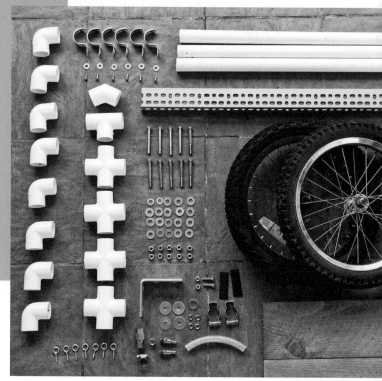

INSTRUCTIONS

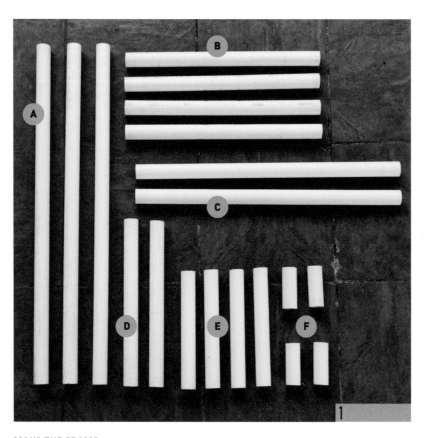

MAKE THE FRAME

1_Cut the three 10' (3 m) PVC pipes into the following segments:

Three 30" (76 cm)	(A)
Four 18" (45.5 cm)	(B)
Two 24" (61 cm)	(C)
Two 14³/₁₆" (36 cm)	(D)
Four 10" (25.5 cm)	(E)
Four 3½" (9 cm)	(F)

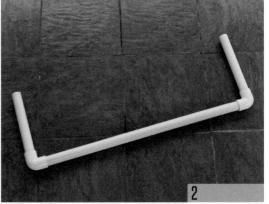

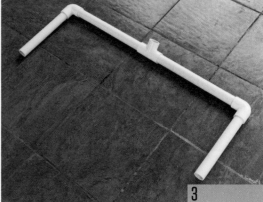

2_Attach an elbow fitting to each end of an A piece. Insert a C piece into each elbow. This will be the rear section of the trailer.

3_Connect the two B pieces with a tee fitting. Attach an elbow fitting to each end of the B pieces. Insert a C piece into each elbow. This will be the front section of the trailer. For now, rotate the tee section so that it points upward by about 45 degrees, as it will be the connection point for the trailer and the hitch arm.

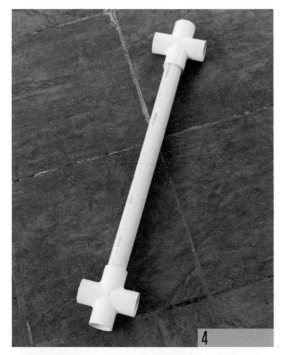

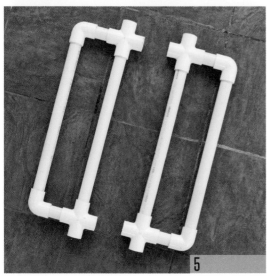

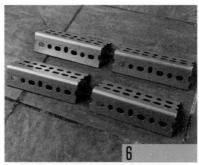

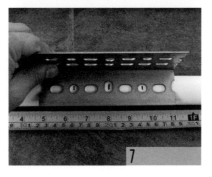

4_Start building the frames that hold the wheels. Select two of the cross fittings and connect them with a D piece. Take another D piece and attach an elbow to each end.

5_Complete the wheel frame by using two E pieces to connect the two D sections you built in the previous steps. Follow steps 4, 5, and 6 again to build a second frame.

6_Now, we'll make the brackets that hold the wheels to the wheel frames. Measure a piece of slotted angle that's long enough to have two bolt holes for mounting to the frame and one hole in the middle for mounting the wheel (mine was approximately 6" [15 cm]). Cut four of these pieces (one for each side of each wheel).

7_Measure and mark the center of each D piece. Center the brackets from step 7 on the D pieces and mark the hole positions for the mounting bolts.

8_Drill all the way through each mounting bolt mark with a ⁵⁄₁₆" (8 mm) drill bit. Make sure that each hole is drilled straight up and down.

9_Using a bolt with a washer on either side, install each bracket with the flats facing inward. Partially thread a locking nylon nut on the bolt, keeping the brackets loose.

10 — Insert each wheel in the bracket holes and tighten the nuts on the wheel spindle. Tighten the locking nylon nuts on each mounting bolt. Double-check that everything is tight and give the wheels a test spin. They should spin freely and nothing should be rubbing anywhere. When the wheels spin freely, disassemble the frames, then reassemble them with primer and glue.

11 — After the glued wheel frames have dried, take the two remaining A pieces, add glue, and connect the wheel frames together as shown. Make sure both wheel frames have the brackets pointing toward the ground before gluing! We'll call this the wheel section.

12 — Disassemble the rear section of the trailer and reassemble with glue, then glue the rear section to the wheel section.

13

13_ Disassemble the front section of the trailer and reassemble with glue, but *do not glue any part of the tee fitting yet.*

—

In the next steps, we'll build the hitch and trailer arm, and we'll need to have those done before the correct angle of the tee on the front piece can be found.

1

2, 3

MAKE THE HITCH AND CONNECTING ARM

1_ Next, we'll make a hitch for the trailer that attaches to your bicycle seatpost. This will take a bit of explaining, so reread the steps as many times as necessary until you understand. The main component of the hitch is a 90-degree strut bracket, which will be attached to the seatpost using two conduit hangers. On the end of the strut bracket is a male quick-connect air fitting, which will allow the trailer to be connected and disconnected quickly and easily.

2_ To make the hitch mount, you'll need a 1" (25 mm)-long ¼" (6 mm) bolt, two ¼" × 1¼" (6 × 32 mm) fender washers, two #10 finishing washers, a ¼" (6 mm) nylon locking nut, a conduit hanger, and the 90-degree four-hole strut bracket. Put the bolt through the hole in the conduit hanger, then put a fender washer on the other side, followed by a finishing washer. Because the bolt's shaft is smaller in diameter than the hole in the strut bracket, the finishing washers are used as spacers to keep the bolt centered in the hole.

3_ Next, put the bolt through a hole in the strut bracket (with the conduit hanger pointing away from the angled strut section), followed by another finishing washer, a fender washer, and the nut. Tighten the bolt, making sure the conduit hanger is pointed so that the hitch will mount parallel with the seat post.

4_ Repeat steps 2 and 3 to attach a second conduit hanger as shown in the photo.

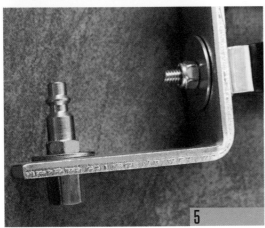

4 _ [OPTIONAL] This optional step will help protect your seatpost from any accidental hitch movement that might scratch it. Remove the tightening bolt from each conduit hanger and slide a piece of heatshrink tubing over each arm of the hanger. Use a tubing dryer or lighter to shrink the heatshrink and form a protective rubber sleeve.

5 _ Take a male quick-connect fitting, put a ½" (13 mm) flat washer over the threads, then put it through the hole in the strut bracket farthest from the conduit hangers. Thread on the ¼" (6 mm) brass pipe cap and tighten it as much as possible to secure it.

6 _ Remove the conduit hanger tightening bolts and test fit the hitch on your bike's seat post (you may need to adjust your seat height). Reinsert the bolts and tighten them so that the hitch can't rotate.

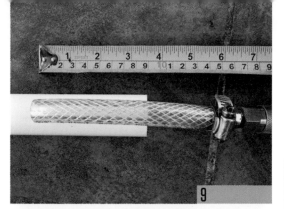

9

7

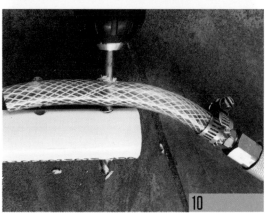

10

8

11

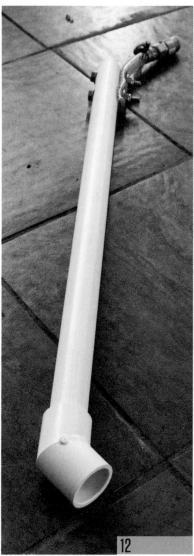

12

7_Now, we'll build the trailer arm! Take the female quick-connect fitting and thread a male quick-connect fitting into the back of it. Tighten the connection as much as possible.

8_Now, take the 6" (15 cm) segment of vinyl tubing, and force it over the end of the male quick-connect fitting. You may need to heat the tubing in hot water to make it a bit more pliable beforehand. Once the tubing is on the fitting, use a pipe clamp to secure it.

9_Set out one of the F pieces. Place the free end of the vinyl tubing on top, overlapping by approximately 3½" (9 cm).

10_Using a ⁵⁄₁₆" (8 mm) drill bit, drill two holes all the way through the tubing and the PVC pipe.

11_Take two 2½" (6.5 cm)-long ⁵⁄₁₆" (8 mm) bolts and secure the tubing to the pipe, using a washer on each side and nylon locking nuts. Tighten the bolts enough that the tube cannot move.

12_Place a 45-degree elbow on the end of the pipe and insert the other F piece into it. Rotate the elbow so that both the vinyl tube and the angle are on the same side. Disassemble and reassemble the pieces with glue.

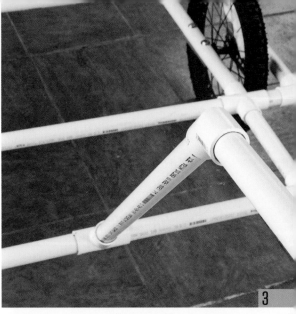

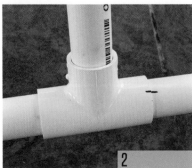

ASSEMBLE THE TRAILER

1_ Now it's time to assemble everything and set the angle of the tee on the front piece of the trailer. Attach the front section of the trailer to the wheel section. Insert the trailer arm into the tee. Attach the trailer arm to the hitch so that everything is connected. *Do not glue anything yet!*

2_ At this point, the trailer might be out of level. Because the tee on the front has not been glued in place, you should be able to adjust its angle. You may also need to shorten the length of the trailer arm that slides into the tee. Once you've adjusted everything so that the trailer is as level as possible, use a marker to mark the position of the tee fitting and the pipe, in relation to each other.

3_ Disassemble the front section of the trailer and reassemble with glue. Make sure the tee is at the correct angle. The hitch arm should be glued into the tee as well.

4_ Once all the glue has dried, take the trailer for a test drive! Make sure everything works as expected and that all bolts are tight and nothing is rubbing.

6 _ Using the six EMT straps, washers and ¾" (19 mm) screws, secure the deck to the pipe as shown in the photo: one in each corner flush against the elbow fittings, and one on either side of the tee in the front section. If desired, add some eye screws to the deck so you can strap or bungee things down and you're done!

5 _ Since the trailer is still just an open frame, you'll likely want to add a deck. Measure the size of the deck you want, and cut a piece of wood to suit. (I chose 33" by 45" [84 cm × 1.14 m].) You'll likely need to cut a notch out of the front for the angled tee piece as well.

FOAM ROCKET LAUNCHER

Supersize your foam dart gun with
a compressed-air foam rocket launcher!
This design can be filled with an ordinary
bike pump and has two tanks so you
get multiple shots. It also has a pressure
regulator, so you can adjust how fast and
far the rocket will launch. The foam
rockets are easy to make, using
duct tape and pool noodles!

TOOLS

PVC PRIMER AND GLUE (AND GLOVES FOR PROTECTION)

RUBBER MALLET

THREAD-SEALING TAPE

ADJUSTABLE WRENCH

MARKER

HACKSAW

DRILL

DRILL BIT
(size dependent on push-button)

ELECTRICAL TAPE

FLATHEAD SCREWDRIVER

LONG KNIFE

BICYCLE PUMP

MATERIALS

FIVE 2" (50 MM) PVC STREET ELBOWS

2" (50 MM) PVC TEE

FOUR PVC REDUCING BUSHING, SPIGOT × FNPT, 2" × ½" (50 × 15 MM) PIPE SIZE

THREE ½" (13 MM) MIP TO ¼" (8 MM) FIP ADAPTERS

⅜" (9 MM) ID TO ½" (13 MM) MIP HOSE BARB

TWO ¼" (6 MM) MIP TO ¼" (6 MM) FIP BRASS BALL VALVES

¼" (6 MM) MIP SCHRADER VALVE

DUCT TAPE

2" (5 CM) PVC ELBOW

2" (5 CM) PVC TO ¾" (20 MM) FIP ADAPTER

¼" (6 MM) MIP CLOSE NIPPLE

¼" (6 MM) FIP AIR-PRESSURE REGULATOR

⅜" (9 MM) ID TO ¼" (6 MM) MIP HOSE BARB

¾" (19 MM) THREADED INLINE ELECTRONIC IRRIGATION VALVE

1¼" (32 MM) PVC TEE

TWO MEDIUM ZIP TIES

5" (12.5 CM) LONG 1¼" (32 MM) PVC PIPE

MOMENTARY PUSH-BUTTON SWITCH WITH LEADS

9-VOLT BATTERY CONNECTOR

9-VOLT BATTERY

1¼" (32 MM) PVC END CAP

¾" (19 MM) MIP BRASS CLOSE NIPPLE

16" (40.5 CM) OF ¾" (20 MM) PVC PIPE

¾" (20 MM) PVC SLIP TO MIP ADAPTER

APPROXIMATELY 40" (1 M) OF ⅜" (9 MM) ID × ½" (12.7 MM) OD BRAIDED VINYL TUBING

TWO ⁵/₁₆" TO ⅞" (8 × 22 MM) STAINLESS STEEL HOSE CLAMPS

ONE POOL NOODLE
(with inner hole about 1" [25 mm] in diameter)

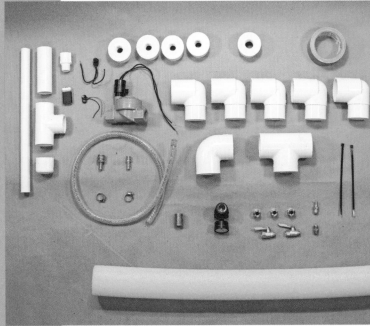

INSTRUCTIONS

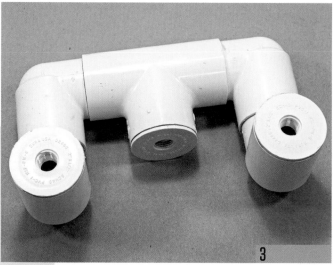

3

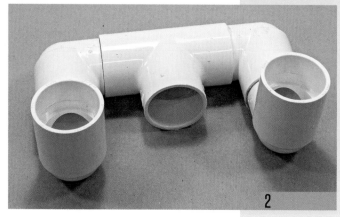

1

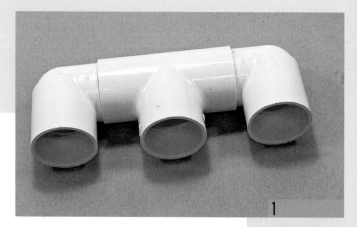

2

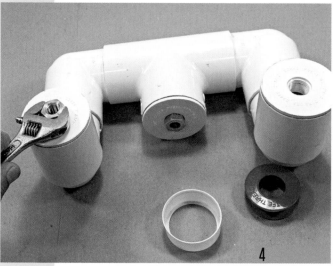

4

3 — Glue a 2" PVC to ½" FIP (50 × 15 mm) adapter into each opening. Allow the glue to set up for at least 15 minutes before going to the next step.

4 — Wrap thread-sealing tape around two of the ½" MIP to ¼" FIP (13 × 6 mm) adapters. Thread one into the middle opening and the other into the opening on the left (as shown in the photo). Tighten them with an adjustable wrench— we don't want any leaks!

BUILD THE PRIMARY TANK

1 — The primary tank will hold most of the air and will allow multiple rocket launches from a single filling. Glue a 2" (50 mm) PVC street elbow into either side of the tee, with the openings pointing in the direction of the tee's middle.

2 — Lay the tank down. Glue two more street elbows into the openings of the first two, with the openings pointing upward.

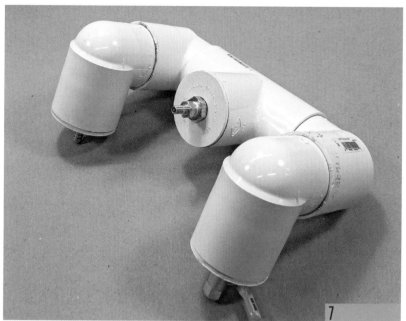

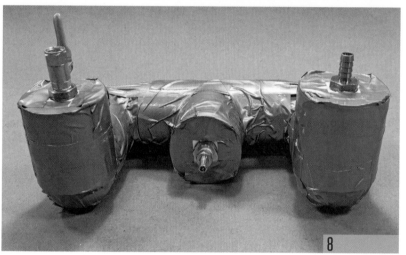

7 — In the middle adapter, apply thread tape and twist in the Schrader valve fitting. This will be where we attach a bike pump for filling the tank.

8 — Make sure everything is good and tight, then wrap the entire tank in a few layers of duct tape. This is just a precautionary measure! If the tank ruptures for any reason (unlikely, with a bike pump), the tape will keep the tank more-or-less intact. Avoid taping over the fittings, of course. The taped tank may not be pretty, but it's safe, and you can always add color later.

5 — Wrap thread-sealing tape around the threads on the ⅜" (9 mm) ID to ½" (13 mm) MIP hose barb threads. Twist the thread into the remaining opening on the right. Tighten this too.

6 — Apply thread-sealing tape to one of the ball valves and twist it into the left adapter. This is the tank "dump valve" which can be used to let pressure out of the tank when you're done.

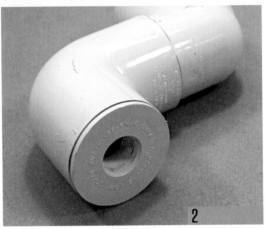

1

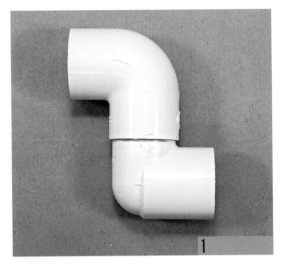

2

3

4

BUILD THE SECONDARY TANK

1_The secondary tank receives regulated pressure from the primary tank, and can be cut off from the primary tank with a ball valve before firing. Glue the remaining street elbow into the 2" (50 mm) PVC elbow, with its opening facing away from the other elbow.

2_Glue the 2" PVC to ¾" FIP adapter into one of the openings. Glue a 2" PVC to ½" FIP (50 × 13 mm) adapter into the other opening. Wait at least 15 minutes for the glue to set up before going to the next step.

3_Apply thread-sealing tape to the last ½" MIP to ¼" FIP (15 × 8 mm) adapter. Thread it into the ½" (15 mm) threaded side of the tank with the wrench.

4_Add thread-sealing tape to both sides of a ¼" (8 mm) close nipple. Twist it into the adapter from step 3, then twist on the pressure regulator with the flow arrow pointing toward the secondary tank.

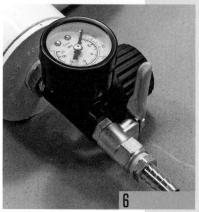

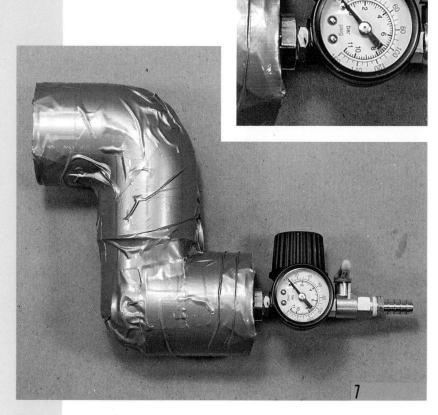

5＿Wrap thread-sealing tape around the male end of the remaining ball valve and tighten it into the free end of the regulator. Make sure the handle can open and shut freely.

6＿Apply thread-sealing tape to the threads of the ⅜" ID to ¼" MIP (9 × 8 mm) hose barb. Tighten it into the ball valve.

7＿Make sure everything is tightened, then wrap the secondary tank in a few layers of duct tape. Take care to leave space around the ¾" (20 mm) threaded hole on the front of the tank.

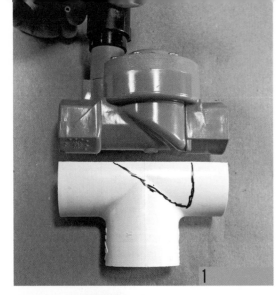

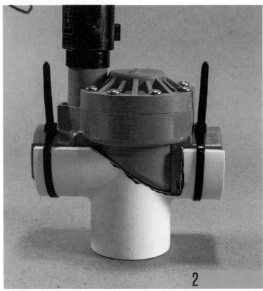

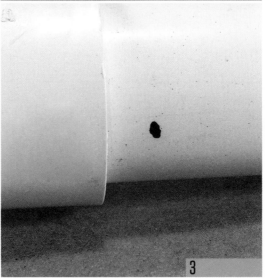

MAKE THE HANDLE AND WIRE UP
THE IRRIGATION VALVE

1_ Cut the 1¼" (32 mm) tee horizontally down the middle, as shown. Hold it up to the bottom of the irrigation valve.

2_ Cut away any middle parts that interfere with the tee fitting securely against the valve. Zip tie the tee to the valve on either side. This will form the base of the handle.

3_ Take the 5" (12.5 cm) piece of 1¼" (32 mm) PVC pipe and stick it into the middle of the tee. Make a mark about ½" (13 mm) from the rim of the tee, and another on the direct opposite side of the pipe.

4_ Remove the section of pipe. Using the correct size drill bit for the button, drill a hole in each mark.

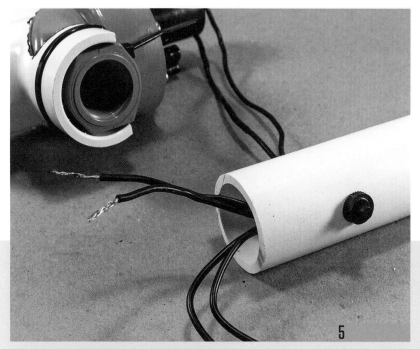

5

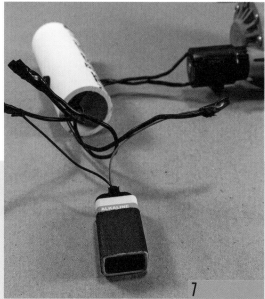

7

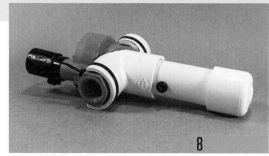

8

6, 7

5 — Insert the button through the hole. Leave the wires sticking out of the pipe. Thread on the button's nut. Stick the irrigation wires through the other hole and out the same side of the pipe.

6 — Twist one of the wires from the button with one of the wires from the irrigation valve. Wrap electrical tape around the connection.

7 — Twist one of the wires from the battery connector to the remaining button wire. Twist the other to the irrigation valve wire. Wrap each of these connections with electrical tape. Connect a 9-volt battery to the holder and push the button to test it. You should hear the valve click open when the button is pushed and click closed when it's released. If it works, push the battery inside the pipe.

8 — Place an end cap on the bottom of the pipe, and then reinsert the pipe in the tee. Since you may have to take this apart in the future, don't glue it. Friction should hold everything together well, but if you need it, use a piece of duct tape.

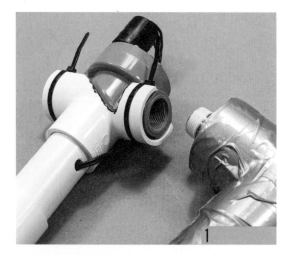

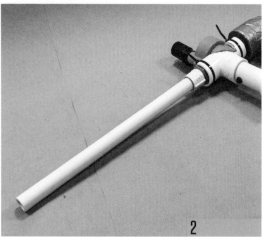

PUT IT ALL TOGETHER

1 _ Apply thread-sealing tape to both sides of the ¾" (20 mm) MIP brass close nipple. Use it to connect the secondary tank to the back of the irrigation valve.

2 _ Take the 16" (40.5 cm)-long ¾" (20 mm) PVC pipe and glue it into the ¾" (20 mm) slip to MIP adapter. Apply thread-sealing tape to the adapter threads. Twist the adapter into the front of the irrigation valve.

3 _ Add a hose clamp to each end of the length of braided vinyl tubing. Use it to connect the two tanks via their hose barbs. Tighten the hose clamps and the rocket launcher is done! Before doing any testing, wait at least 2 hours for all the glue joints set up fully.

4 _ If you like, decorate the launcher and tanks with different colors of duct tape! To make them easy to carry, I also added belt loops made from duct tape folded over on itself.

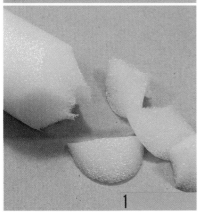

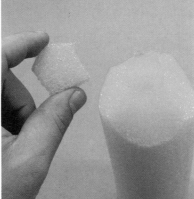

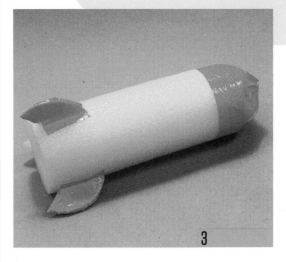

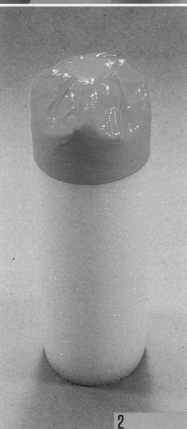

MAKE A FOAM ROCKET

1_Set out a pool noodle. Use a knife to cut off a section 10 to 12" (25.5 to 30.5 cm) long. This will be the foam rocket body. Use the knife to shave down one end. Save any large pieces that result for the next step.

2_ Take one of the larger pieces and cut it so that it will fit and function as a plug in the middle of the rocket. Once it's in, wrap a cross of duct tape over the end, then wrap around the cross a couple of times. Take a deep breath and blow into the back of the rocket to make sure that it forms a decent seal!

3_ If you like, add fins to the back of the rocket using duct tape and strips of foam. If the rocket doesn't fly straight, undo the front tape and add a bit of weight inside, then retape it. This will help shift the rocket's center of gravity forward so it flies straighter. Feel free to experiment with other modifications and designs!

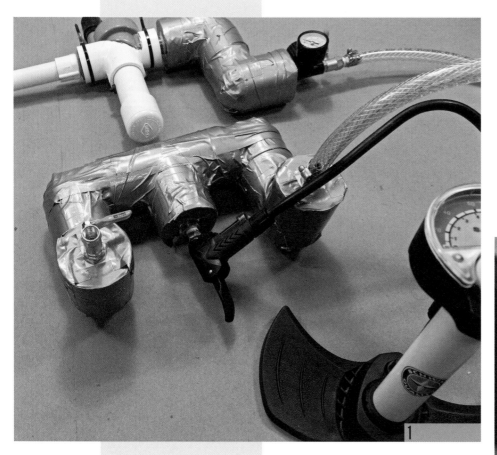

FIRING ROCKETS

1—Close the primary tank ball valve. Hook up the bike pump to the Schrader valve.

2—Pump up the tank to approximately 60 to 75 psi (4 to 5 bar) (don't exceed 80 psi [5.5 bar]!). Detach the bike pump.

3—Adjust the regulator to about 15 to 20 psi (1 to 1.4 bar). Close the ball valve on the secondary tank.

4—Stick a foam rocket onto the end of the barrel. Push the button to fire it! To fire another shot, just open the secondary tank's ball valve to fill it, then shut it again. If you want a more powerful shot, open the ball valve and adjust the regulator to a higher psi before shutting it again.

ABOUT THE AUTHOR

Jordan Bunker is a San Francisco Bay–area engineer, designer, artist, and craftsman who relishes taking on ambitious projects with short timescales.

—

He has also been a fabricator, hat salesman, journalist, and documentarian (among many, many other things). His hobbies include vintage Volvo repair, making sawdust, and drinking coffee. You can find more of his past and current projects on his website at www.hierotechnics.com.

—

Jordan believes that the most important feeling that can be passed to others is a sense of curiosity and a desire to connect with (and modify!) the world around us.

ACKNOWLEDGMENTS

Just as most big projects are made easier by having extra hands, this book benefitted from the assistance of many people working behind the scenes. Thanks are in order to Lindsay and Jim for helping me shoot photos and for putting up with general project mayhem around the house. A huge thank-you also to Judith, Anne, and the rest of the publishing team for bringing it all together.

INDEX

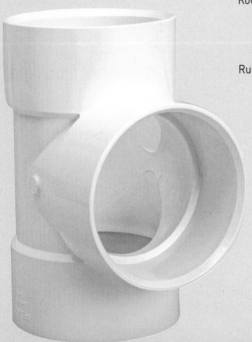

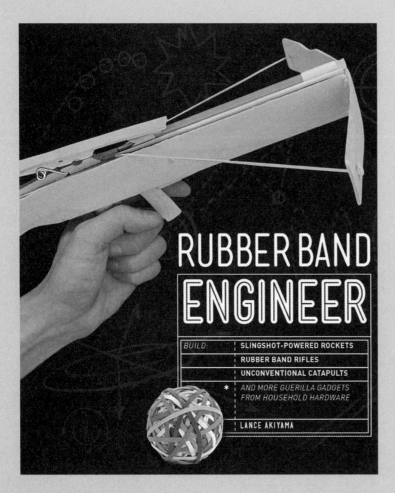

RUBBER BAND ENGINEER
978-1-63159-104-4

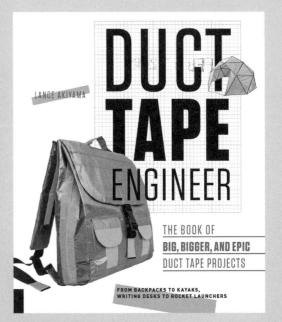

DUCT TAPE ENGINEER
978-1-63159-130-3

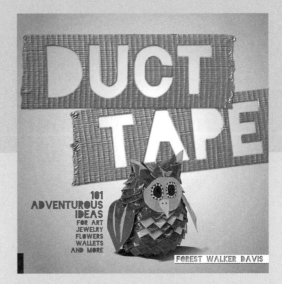

Duct Tape
978-1-63159-016-0